BEHIND THE GREEN CARD

BEHIND THE GREEN CARD

HOW IMMIGRATION POLICY IS KILLING THE AMERICAN DREAM

DONALD S. DOBKIN, LL.B., LL.M.

Algora Publishing
New York

Library of Congress Cataloging-in-Publication Data —

Dobkin, Donald S.
    Behind the green card : how immigration policy is killing the American
dream / Donald S. Dobkin, LL.B., LL.M.
       pages cm
    Includes bibliographical references and index.
    ISBN 978-0-87586-969-8 (soft cover: alk. paper) —ISBN 978-0-87586-
970-4 (hard cover: alk. paper) —ISBN 978-0-87586-971-1 (ebook) 1. Emigration
and immigration law—United States. 2. United States—Emigration and
immigration—Government policy. I. Title.
    KF4819.D63 2013
    325.73—dc23
                                    2013004879

Printed in the United States

Finally a book on immigration by someone who's actually done it—not a journalist, not a think tank, not a career academic. Donald Dobkin surgically dissects the key elements of our immigration structure and explains in a highly readable style why we have the problems we do and the difficult prospects for solving them. Dobkin has hit the ball off the cover with this important book. — **Rami Fakhoury, Founder, Fakhoury Law Group**

Behind the Green Card is a must read for students and practitioners of immigration law and social scientists more generally. Donald Dobkin's book provides an exhaustive account of the law and unintended consequences that surface in the wake of this dysfunctional legal system. Dobkin should be applauded for combining a scholarly understanding of the issues with a practitioner's practical eye towards addressing them. — **Robert Koulish, Ph.D. Professor of Political Science, University of Maryland**

Just because someone – especially an immigration lawyer - can write a book, doesn't mean it's worth reading. It may just mean they know the mechanics of book writing. *Behind The Green Card* isn't just another homogenized self-serving publication from just another member of the cautious, money-clutching herd. This book is part history and part policy discussion. But most important to me is it's compelling descriptions of abuses of power and overly far-reaching authority within the US government immigration machinery.

In 1771, Edmund Burke said "The greater the power, the more dangerous the abuse." Dobkin's *Behind The Green Card* is a refreshing and welcome view into the current morass of immigration law. Dobkin isn't afraid to question anything: the economically debilitating immigration business legal system, a disturbing quasi-lawmaking in the executive branch, an oddly Schutzstaffel-like ICE security force, and the erosion of due process. Nothing escapes his discerning and penetrating net, including the expedient interests of politician and bureaucrats like.

Here's what's dangerous: Americans being so contented, soft, and complacent that the government can run amok without anyone being very concerned. Here's what's dangerous in Immigration Law: lawyers making enough money, properly and otherwise (encouraged by their organizations?) to ignore any path to a reasonable and beneficial immigration legal system. Finally there is a book that carries that actuality out of its dark shadow – this one.

Behind The Green Card is a sturdy rudder for guidance toward 1) a better immigration scheme; 2) a government guided by principals; and 3) an ethical foundation for immigration lawyers. If that doesn't interest you, don't buy it - there's always NPR, Fox News, or another CIR webinar. — **Anthony Guidice, Esq. ILW.COM**

To David

No book is just the work of one person. And this book is no different. In fact, this work really began in theory in 1975, the year I left Canada to attend graduate school in the United States.

My impressions of the United States and its immigration system then are markedly different than my impressions today. My book will highlight those changes.

I want to thank a number of people who made a difference along the way. First and foremost, my advisor at Johns Hopkins, Prof. Joel Grossman in the Department of Political Science, a true icon in law and politics, the Supreme Court and public law in general. Joel has supported and encouraged my research and writing from the beginning. I also want to thank another Hopkins professor in the Political Science department, Prof. Joe Cooper, another icon of American political science. Joe has also encouraged me from the beginning. Lastly, I want to thank the Johns Hopkins University itself, for offering me a university scholarship and introducing me to the world of academic scholarship. And finally, I want to acknowledge the contribution of Prof. Victor Rosenblum, my graduate advisor at Northwestern Law School, who has since passed away.

Special thanks to my longtime research assistant, Kyle Landis-Marinello, a gifted University of Michigan law school graduate and Rhodes finalist. Kyle has been an invaluable member of my team from the beginning and is now well on his way to establishing a very successful legal career.

Additional thanks to Rami Fakhoury and the Fakhoury Law Group. Rami has supported me and been my confidant in all matters concerning immigration since I met up with him in 2004.

TABLE OF CONTENTS

INTRODUCTION

I decided to write a book on immigration for several reasons, not the least of which was the belief that the American public was not getting the true story about our immigration system. Books about immigration have typically come from the ranks of journalists, think tanks, politicians and academics. I practiced immigration law for 30 years. I spent my professional life in the trenches and thought it worthwhile to share my perspective. I witnessed up front and firsthand what a disaster the system is. Virtually everyone I hear on the talk shows, or talk to in person, hasn't a clue about how the system really functions. Misconceptions and misinformation rule the day. Mayor Michael Bloomberg of New York City has described America's immigration policy as the greatest case of national suicide ever seen. It's time for someone who actually did it to tell the American people the facts about our immigration system.

The U.S. is no longer the only game in town. We need to get off of our arrogant pedestal. America's hard line toward immigration has sent applicants fleeing to other countries. India, Canada, Australia, New Zealand and the U.K. have benefited enormously from this flight. The economic consequences of this policy have been severe. We have an economy that cannot mount a serious recovery because in large part we have killed the demand, by killing immigration. Canada allows four times the amount of immigrants on a per capita basis than does the U.S. Look into what type of home you can buy in Toronto or Vancouver with a million dollars. You would be shocked to discover how little a million dollars buys in either of these cities, and I doubt you would want to live in the million dollar home! Why? Because demand drives prices and economies. And mass immigration to both of these Canadian cities has been the principal reason for their strong property markets. Contrast this with U.S. home prices, which continue their free fall in all but a few select regions. There simply is not enough demand to buy all of these properties, largely because we don't have enough immigration.

The U.S. Court of Appeals has noted that immigration law is a very complex subject. It remarked, "With only a small degree of hyperbole, the immigration laws have been termed "second only to the Internal Revenue Code in complexity."[1] My book is not about being pro-immigration or anti-immigration. I am neither a Democrat nor a Republican. I am an independent who has voted about equally for both parties over the years. However, I am the first to concede my strong belief that there are significant economic benefits (and others) to accommodative immigration.

This book is all about giving you, the reader, snapshots of the immigration process. The book is organized into a series of "vignettes," as it were, giving you unique glimpses of the immigration system, glimpses and background you will not get anywhere else. When I started practicing immigration law over 30 years ago, the "culture of no" was in existence, but the government often gave applicants for visas the benefit of the doubt. Today, the attitude has become one of "how can we reject you and find a reason to send you home, or never let you get here in the first place." A U.S. Chamber of Commerce sponsored event in 2012 underscored the visa challenges facing multinational giants. Companies described their L-1 intracompany visa woes to USCIS Director Alejandro Mayorkas, reporting that they do not have the needed flexibility to deploy

---

1 *Castro-O'Ryan v. INS*, 847 F.2d 1307, 1312 (9th Cir. 1988).

professional resources to the U.S. for various projects, whether in the manufacturing sector or the information technology arena. The bottom line: adjudicatory standards have tightened in the absence of any legislative action or pronounced Agency policy change.

At a recent job fair conducted in the U.S. by Canadian high tech companies, officers from Immigration Canada accompanied the recruiters to the fairs. Job applicants to whom offers were made were granted visas to Canada on the spot. To my knowledge, U.S. immigration officers have never accompanied American corporate recruiters to job fairs, nor have they ever granted a U.S. immigration visa in this fashion. And in the present environment, such co-operation between government and industry would be impossible to fathom. In fact, corporate behemoths such as Exxon Mobil have virtually given up trying to get foreign personnel into the country and have set up offshore centers in London and elsewhere.

Microsoft, several years back, opened a high tech center in Vancouver. Foreign companies who need to send technical people into the U.S. to service their U.S. customers and supervise the installation of equipment have also found it virtually impossible to get visas. We spend millions educating foreign Ph.D.s, then deny them a path to obtain legal residence. Something is radically wrong and we need to do something fast to correct it.

The idyllic dream of comprehensive immigration reform is a red herring, indeed. Oddly enough, despite campaign promises to the contrary, President Obama has done next to nothing to reform the immigration arena. Even when the Democrats controlled the Congress in the first two years of his administration, immigration was not a priority. Blame the obstinate Republication hard liners for his failure to get anywhere? Sure, that has something to do with it. But the President could have by the power of executive order changed 50% of the existing immigration rules and procedures by a stroke of the pen. His recent Executive Order staying the deportations of students who had been here practically since birth, is a welcome step, however, it is mostly an election band-aid. After all, isn't he the titular head of the Department of Homeland Security? Hasn't the Congress delegated the job of creating definitions and rules to the agency? And doesn't the President have the authority and indeed the responsibility of setting policy?

We need to focus our attention on three main areas. First is to overhaul the legal immigration categories to favor highly educated professionals and successful entrepreneurs. Second, we need to deal with the 12 million or so illegal immigrants by providing a realistic, not draconian, path to legal residence. As Jack Welch, the former CEO of General Electric has said, "Immigration isn't just an economic issue.... It's a managerial one, and any plan that suggests that the U.S. deport illegal workers violates one of management's cardinal rules: You have to face reality." And lastly, we need a new culture at the Department of Homeland Security, one that encompasses the role of visa facilitator, not visa obstructionist.

The economic reality is that Medicare, Medicaid and Social Security are bankrupt. We are spending $130 million an hour more than we take in. Our national debt, including off balance sheet liabilities, exceeds $100 trillion. There are limits to how much one can abuse the privilege of being the world's reserve currency. England found that out after World War II. Despite the demagogues on both sides of the aisle in the Congress, we need millions of new immigrants to pay into these programs to have any hope of saving them. We need to wake up before the music stops. We are running out of time.

1. The Diminishing Prospects for Legal Immigration

It began at 6:00 a.m. on June 1, 1980, when 21,000 Cuban refu-gees confined to their barracks at the U.S. Army base in Ft. Chaffee, Arkansas, began to riot. Buildings were set ablaze as three hundred refugees escaped into the neighboring towns of Barling and Ft. Smith.

William ("Bill") J. Clinton, then-Governor of Arkansas, was awakened with the bad news. The Arkansas National Guard was ordered into action as Clinton arrived on the scene. Clinton took command of the situation immediately. "I don't want any of our people hurt," he said firmly. "I'm not telling you how to do your jobs, but I want it understood that if anybody is injured, I want it to be the Cubans..."[1] Looking straight at his commander, he added, "Am I making myself clear?"

The events of that steamy summer morning left an indelible impression on the future 42nd President of the United States and would mark the beginning of the current cycle of ever tightening rules and policies restricting legal immigration. Although much of the focus on immigration restrictions began during George W.

---

1 Jack Moseley, *"Clinton Tested By Cubans and Politics,"* ARK. NEWS BUREAU, June 3, 2005, http://www.arkansasnews.com/archive/2005/06/03/JackMoseley/322081. html .

Bush's administration, it was during the Clinton Administration that reactionary policies toward immigration actually began.

Since that time, the INS, now split into ICE (enforcement branch) and USCIS (immigration services), has made it increasingly difficult for foreign nationals to legally immigrate. Because of these draconian policies, projected numbers of illegal immigrants have actually increased rather than decreased. Like the failure of the "war on drugs" to actually reduce or prevent trafficking, restrictive reform has only served to feed the necessity for immigration outside the law.

The Illegal Immigration Reform Act

During President Clinton's administration and at his urging, Congress passed the Illegal Immigration Reform Act of 1996. Despite its seemingly direct title, the act was actually devoted to significantly restricting legal immigration, not just reforming the myriad policies attendant to it. In the name of these restrictions, the act has fostered "a series of bad policy choices that have destroyed families, made it virtually impossible to permit illegal immigrants to become legal, and rendered our legal system impotent to stop ... abuses by government officials who may now run amok without any judicial oversight."[1]

Rather than do much in the way of creating effective reform, the Act of 1996 has actually served only to confuse and complicate the process of legal immigration, especially regarding those seeking political asylum, restricting access of immigrants to apply for political asylum by giving officials the unfettered right to deport would-be refugees upon arrival, while those not deported are required to apply for political asylum within one year or render themselves ineligible. In many cases, refugees were more likely to remain in the United States illegally rather than risk asylum denial and deportation, especially if they were unable to file for asylum in a timely matter.

---

1 Ira Kurzban, "Without Review, President Becomes King," *Sun Sentinel*, (Sept. 30, 2006), http://articles.sun-sentinel.com/2006-09-30/news/0609290356_1_illegal-immigration-reform-judicial-review-mandatory-detention>

Later on, the act was amended to generate new restrictions for those on temporary visas who applied for green cards or permanent residence, creating a host of new standards and regulations that must be met for immigrants with different abilities and/or reasons for application. With this amendment, aliens were only allowed to adjust status if they maintained lawful status, or otherwise be deported.

Ironically, the law also made it incredibly difficult to maintain lawful status by creating a new host of bureaucracy and lengthy processes that must be completed in order to be a "lawful" alien.

Firstly, the amendment prohibited aliens who were out of status for even a day to lawfully adjust their status and barred aliens who were out of status for more than three months from applying for a visa at a U.S. Embassy abroad for three years. Those who maintained illegal status for more than a year were barred from application for ten years. Rather than provide options for legal adjustment of status toward these immigrants (who may have been trying to remain here legally — bewildered by the complex and arduous process of maintaining status), an incentive to remain here illegally was created as suddenly many immigrants were ineligible for legal immigration and forced to leave.

As an alien outside of the United States has no legal rights or standing to seek relief in federal courts, immigrants who were out of status for even a day were left with few options. This "court stripping" procedure was created to produce outcomes at less cost, a neoliberal strategy that purportedly expedites the legal process while also clearly sacrificing individual rights and fair process.[1]

In yet another catch-22, the act also asserted that applicants who returned home after their temporary visas expired and then applied for immigration status, legally, demonstrated an intent to become permanent residents, which rendered them ineligible. Even if immigrants did not intend on becoming permanent residents during their initial application for a temporary visa, they could not be accepted.

---

1 Koulish, Robert. *Immigration and American Democracy: Subverting the Rule of Law*, Routledge: New York, 2010, at 8.

The amendment also stripped federal courts of jurisdiction over virtually all late amnesty applications, resulting in thousands of aliens being unable to extend their employment status, resulting in unemployment, while also requiring that those who filed for visas for relatives take on financial responsibility for those same applicants now rendered unemployed.

While federal appeals courts could no longer review denials of various types of relief, including voluntary departure and adjustment of status, it also substantially narrowed the legal definition of refugee. According to the law, only a person who had been forced to abort a pregnancy or undergo involuntary sterilization, or had been subject to other population control programs, could enter the U.S. and legally receive refugee status.[1]

Rather than allow qualified foreign medical professionals to enter the U.S., the amendment required doctors who sought waivers of the two-year foreign residence requirement to work in areas lacking medical professionals for no less than three years.[2]

Further, foreign RNs were now required to pass the Commission on Graduates of Foreign Nursing Schools, even when licensed to practice in states that did not require the exam.[3] Rather than admitting more medical professionals, even when needed, this amendment limited the number of applicants while also restricting those who would legally practice medicine.

At each turn, the Immigration Reform Act under the Clinton administration made the process more complex for legal immigrations. Rather than merely tightening policy or improving infrastructure, the burden was firmly shifted to immigrants to wade through layers of complex regulations and deadlines, filing for legal status in an often unattainable timeframe while following arbitrary procedures.

In short, the law made it far easier to immigrate illegally than legally — the exact opposite of the desired effect.

---

1 8 U.S.C. § 1101(a)(42).
2 8 U.S.C. § 1182.
3 8 U.S.C. § 1182(a)(5)(C).

"Give Us Your Best & Brightest"

The Immigration Act of 1990 allowed aliens to obtain visas if doing so would serve United States' "national interest."[1] Exceptional abilities would exempt applicants from the requirement that they obtain a job offer from a U.S. employer before application. However, the failure of Congress to define "national interest" left the door wide open for the INS to do so, once again giving that agency a vast source of unchecked power.

Subsequently, the INS set forth strict limitations, requiring at least three of the following criteria be met:[2]

1. An official academic record of degree, diploma, certificate, or award
2. Letters of recommendation that showed alien had at least ten years of full-time experience
3. License to practice the profession or certification for a particular profession or occupation
4. A salary or other remuneration that demonstrates exceptional ability
5. Membership in professional associations

Recognition for achievements and significant contributions to the industry or field by peers, government entities, or professional business organizations

Even though these criteria, although arduous, might have been effective in identifying immigrants of outstanding ability, remarkably, this definition had little to do with the Act of 1990 itself. In fact, the INS only defined "national interest" when issuing a decision within the N.Y. *State Dep't of Transportation* appeals case of 1998, stating that:

1. The applicant must be seeking employment in an area of "substantial intrinsic merit."
2. The proposed benefit had to be in national scope.
3. The applicant seeking exemption from the labor certification requirement must present a national benefit so

---

1 Immigration and Nationality Act of 1990, Pub. L. 101-649, § 121, 104 Stat. 4978 (codified as amended at 8 U.S.C. § 1153(b)(2)(B) (2006)).
2 See 8 C.F.R § 204.5(k)(1)(ii) (2006).

great as to outweigh the national interest seeking labor certification.[1]

This language allowed the INS to subjectively and unilaterally assess and evaluate any applicant and determine by its own standards (some might say "whims") which aliens' achievements were worthy of admittance and/or waivers of requirements.

Unfortunately, this was just another instance of failure by both the courts and the agencies to set forth affective provisions in dealing with visa distribution. In 1984, the Supreme Court decision of *Chevron, U.S.A., Inc. v. Natural Resources Defense Council* defined interpretation of "statutory source" in regard to documentation fraud. In other words, statutory provisions would be interpreted by agencies rather than courts, giving excessive power to agencies.

Moreover, the *Chevron* case is the most cited in U.S. history — more than *Roe v. Wade*, *Marbury v. Madison*, *Brown v. Board of Education*, or other historic Supreme Court cases.[2] It is constantly used to uphold arbitrary agency power in instances where legal definition and recourse should exist.

Immigration in the Post 9/11 Era

It's surprising to note that prior to 9/11, as governor of Texas, George W. Bush was considered pro-immigration by virtue of his close association with the substantial base of Hispanic constituents in Texas.[3] In the 2000 election, he garnered 40 percent of the Hispanic vote. As he ascended to the Presidency in January 2001, he could not have anticipated the degree to which immigration policy would take center stage later that year.

Unfortunately, after 9/11, scrutiny fell upon the new President for his "lax" attitude towards immigration, and in order to combat this reputation, reactionary decisions had to be made. And startling action was taken. During these turbulent days, the INS as it was then constituted was about to die.

1 *In re* N.Y. *State Dep't of Transp.*, No. 3363, 22 I. & N. Dec. 215 (B.I.A. 1998).
2 Stephen G. Breyer, et al., *Administrative Law And Regulatory Policy: Problems, Text, And Cases* 290 (5th ed. 2002)
3 Jim Yardley, "The 2000 Campaign: The Texas Governor; Hispanics Give Attentive Bush Mixed Reviews," *New York Times*, Aug. 27, 2000, § 1, at 11.

When it was revealed that an al-Qaeda ring leader received a renewal of his student visa some months after the attacks, despite his death in those attacks,[1] media scrutiny turned to the INS, tightening restrictions.

Reacting to public furor, in April 2002 the Commissioner of the INS testified before Congress that he had instituted a "zero tolerance policy"[2] towards immigration officers, which made many officers extremely anxious but did nothing to improve immigration bureaucracy or even to significantly affect national security.

Rather than manage the process as it existed, officers began to send Requests for Evidence (RFEs) to applicants, creating a huge backlog in applications and mountains of new and daunting paperwork. In response to the backlogs of applications as the machine relentlessly ground to near halt, the INS then instituted the policy of allowing officers to deny applications outright, without even the requirement to issue RFEs.

Of course, people became angrier and more frustrated on all fronts: overburdened consular officers, the media, the immigrants, and even the American public. After a few months, it became clear the "zero tolerance" policy was not working and had no chance to work in the future.

Several regulatory changes began to take place as well. One of the most significant was related to labor certification. The Department of Labor published regulations overhauling the Labor Certification process whereby employers test the U.S. job market to ensure that there are no qualified U.S. workers for the position being sought by the alien.[3] In cases where immigrants were offered jobs while still outside the U.S., they had to obtain certification from the Department of Labor that the position could not be filled by a qualified U.S. worker before the alien could receive an approved visa.

---

1 David Johnston, "A Nation Challenged: The Hijackers, 6 Months Later, I. N. S. Notifies Flight School of Hijackers' Visas," *New York Times*, Mar. 13, 2002, at A16.

2 Thomas, supra note 76, at 1.

3 Immigration and Nationality Act, Pub. L. 101-649, §212, 104 Stat. 4978 (codified as amended at 8 U.S.C. § 1182(a)(5)(A) (2006)).

The Department of Labor also created a set of labor certification regulations called "PERM" (Program Electronic Review Management), which became effective March 27, 2005.

PERM attempted to change regulation by simplifying processes and reducing the backlogs in processing at the various regional offices of the Department of Labor.[1] It allowed employers to do the required recruitment of U.S. workers in advance of filing the actual Labor Certification application.[2] In addition, these new regulations granted certifying officers the ability to revoke approved certifications at any time within five years of approval.[3]

While these steps may have simplified the processing of visa applications, they also have significantly reduced rates of approval, reducing the number of immigrants with work visas and also requiring employers to recruit U.S. workers before offering jobs to those (perhaps more qualified) overseas.

Like other acts since the Clinton era, rather than improving regulations for legal immigration, these changes have only served to incidentally encourage illegal immigration while also generating the need for some U.S. companies to move high-qualification jobs out of this country.

Despite all the controversy, President Bush's administration yielded little new immigration legislation. Principally, we got the Homeland Security Act, creating the Department of Homeland Security and replacing INS with three new divisions within DHS: U.S. Immigration and Customs Enforcement ("ICE"), Customs and Border Protection ("CBP"), and the Citizenship and Immigration Services ("CIS").[4] These minor changes were largely cosmetic, with little impact on immigration law.

More Barriers — More Bureaucracy

New policies have dramatically diminished the possibility for legal immigration, while escalating the population of illegal im-

---

1 See Francis E. Chin, *U.S. Fast Tracks Employment-Based Immigration: Proceed With Caution*, 49 B.B.J. 14 (2005).
2 Program Electronic Review Management, 69 Fed. Reg. at 77327.
3 Department of Labor, "Frequently Asked Questions," http://www.ows.doleta.gov/foreign/faqsanswers.asp (last visited Nov. 1, 2006).
4 Id. §§ 251, 271, 275, 291.

migrants. Comparable to the seemingly futile war on drugs, these innumerable new regulations have actually overwhelmed legal activity by overcomplicating regulations. Over the past decade, over 2 million illegal immigrants have been deported from the United States. From 2001 to 2010, the total number of immigrants who pass through ICE detention per year has also nearly doubled, from 209,000 individuals in 2001 to almost 392,000 individuals in 2010.[1] Many millions of illegal immigrants reside in this country despite more and more laws and ever greater enforcement intended to bar them.

Clearly, something is not working.

---

1 Dep't of Homeland Security, U.S. Immigration and Customs Enforcement, Immigration Enforcement Actions: 2010 (June 2011), available at http://www.dhs.gov/xlibrary/assets/statistics/publications/enforcement-ar-2010.pdf [hereafter "Immigration Enforcement Actions: 2010"]

2. The Best and Brightest — Where Has All the Talent Gone?

> *"America needs a policy that encourages skilled workers and*
> *people with exceptional abilities to come to our country. Unfortunate-*
> *ly, our current system discourages them from immigrating..."*
> — *Senator Jesse Helms, U.S. Senate, July 12, 1989*

Senator Helms had it right when he crafted the National Inter-est Waiver/Exceptional Ability Category in the Immigration Act of 1990. Helms described the transformation that took place in North Carolina as "truly remarkable," as he witnessed the shift from a dying tobacco economy to one led and transformed by foreign PhDs and MDs who had emigrated to work and live in Research Triangle, NC.

Senator Helms' ideas on immigration and what it could ac-complish for America were hardly what one would expect from a staunch conservative. He foresaw, decades before the challenges we now face, that America would be engaged in fierce worldwide competition for scientific, technological, engineering, research and industrial talent.

By considering this legislation, the Congress's intent was to en-courage foreign nationals holding advanced degrees and possessing specialized capabilities to come to the United States. The law recognized a primary need to remain competitive and at the cutting edge of research and development across a vast range of industries and initiatives. Despite this early effort and directly due to the dizzying array of contradictory laws and policies enacted since then, far too few scientists have come to this country since 1990.

Of the 1,107,126 persons who immigrated to the United States in 2008 (USCIS Statistical Yearbook, 2008) only 1,214 persons were admitted under the Exceptional Ability Category. The history is shocking:

Year	Number of Immigrants
1999	838
2000	1857
2001	6533
2002	5323
2003	2437
2004	1400
2005	1488
2006	972
2007	1171
2008	1214

Numbers in the ensuing years are progressively dismal. In short, the United States is ceding its premier position as a world leader in scientific development and technological advances. We are losing the battle for great minds by embracing policies which make it virtually impossible for those persons to enter our country. The warnings are ominous and growing:

> "China is now the second largest producer of scientific knowledge and is on course to overtake the U.S. by 2020." — Thompson Reuters

> "China far outperformed every other nation, with a 64-fold increase in peer-reviewed scientific papers since 1981." — *Financial Times*, January 26, 2001

So what happened? Why have so few applicants qualified for this category since its enactment in 1990? You need only to look to the INS for the answers, and those answers will make you cringe.

In the early 1990s, the INS was deluged with applications under the "exceptional" category, and agency approvals struggled to keep up with the demand. This result — precisely the outcome desired by the law — did not sit well with the Clinton Administration. Worse yet, in 1998 the Wall Street Journal ran a front page article mocking the INS for approving virtually "anyone with a pulse" under the category. The WSJ article cited examples of "an acrobat from Russia who plays a horn while flying through the air, Korean golf course designers, Russian ballroom dancers and Ghanaian drum makers," and the INS had had enough. That very month, the INS issued a precedent decision regarding NY State Department of Transportation and the law died, murdered by inept public relations, despite the limitless benefits it might accrue.

Not even a decade after the creation of the "exceptional" category, the INS killed it due to acute case of embarrassment. Rather than address the issues and amend its procedures, the INS *policed* itself into submission, and the U.S. has unknowingly suffered for that suicide-by-regulation ever since.

When considering the overheated immigration problem in the United States, it's important to remember that America is a country virtually founded on a history of successful politicians, scientists, and entrepreneurs who came to our country from foreign soil. The hysterical tirades claiming that America is exclusively for Americans fail to note that the North American continent is populated primarily by immigrants — and very successful, thriving immigrants at that.

As of 2000, Chinese or Indian immigrants made up 29% of Silicon Valley technology companies, with total revenue amounting to $19.5 billion and over 70,000 jobs created.[1]

---

1 Becklumb, Peggy; "Canada's Immigration Program," *Parliamentary Information and Research Services*; September 10 2008, http://www2.parl.gc.ca/content/lop/researchpublications/bp190-e.pdf

Many groundbreaking politicians, diplomats and activists have been immigrants, and our culture has been enriched by artists and thinkers who were born overseas. Historically, a significant part of the American dream entailed creating something out of nothing, the destitute immigrant landing on the shores of opportunity, fashioning success by the sheer forces of will, talent and hard work. We embraced and celebrated those hardy souls brave enough to leave countries stricken by war and poverty by giving them opportunities to create a better life, not just for themselves but toward the progression of the United States as a center for global advancement in innovation and capital. It is a fair guess to offer that your own family has one or more stories of rags to riches which perfectly fit this category.

In recent years, the U.S. has steadily scaled back support for immigration, including skilled and unskilled workers desperately needed in our country, allowing America to fall dangerously behind in the global competition for intelligence and capital, contributing to a climate of poisonous economic decline.

After 9/11, immigration policy has slammed the door shut on brainpower, especially concerning foreign-born college students. From 2001–2003, the number of student visas fell from over 6 million to 2.7 million.[1] Even more daunting for students is the virtually nonexistent prospect of continuing their education at the PhD level or accepting jobs in their fields of expertise. By inhibiting and sometimes prohibiting advanced students from achieving permanent immigrant status, we allow our universities to invest millions in the education of these students, only to send those brains away once they have achieved advanced qualifications, actively choosing not to reap the benefits of our own higher education systems.

At every turn, we've made it increasingly difficult for academics and entrepreneurs to obtain green cards and choked the number of entry level jobs for immigrants as the number of native-born college educated students in these positions continues to rise. Meanwhile, ominous warning signs loom larger as other countries who have

---

1 Becklumb, *Ibid.*

implemented sensible and productive immigration policies have prospered.

The United States is not the only country to have been built and defined by mass migration. Canada and Australia are European settlements that came to be industrialized, first-world countries much in the same way.[1] Since the 1970s, these countries have expanded efforts into carefully selecting their immigrant population, rather than restricting it. Rather than view immigration as restrictive first and foremost, they view possible immigrants as opportunities to increase their own country's productivity and potential.

These nations have also maintained some of the lowest populations of undocumented immigrants in comparison to other capitalist countries. Currently the total population of immigrants for Australia is 22%; Canada is 21%, and the United States scores among the lowest of the Western world with a total of 14%, followed only by Germany (13%), Britain (10%), and Italy (7%). Meanwhile, the United States bears a population of undocumented immigrants in the tens of millions.

At a time of rising unemployment across the board, as well as a time where a War on Terror perpetuates the view of foreigners as enemy, reactionary politics have strangled sensible policy with the intention of slowing immigration blindly, with little consideration of the benefits earlier policies have afforded us. By examining Australia and Canada, countries that have made alternate choices and reaped untold benefits, we can see the benefits of progressive immigration reform, especially in the areas of scientific, technological, medical, academic and other forms of innovation.

The United States, when compared to smaller European countries, is much stricter regarding immigration policy; it is blinding itself to skills that could benefit our country's position globally and economically. Instead of strategically crafting policy that attracts foreign entrepreneurs, scientific innovators, and students, we try to keep everyone out, forcing too many people who might otherwise benefit the U.S. to choose between other nations or living here illegally.

---

1 http://www.cbsa-asfc.gc.ca/agency-agence/stca-etps-eng.html#d01

While other nations give priority to immigrants with enough ambition, capital and talent to stimulate job creation and global competitiveness, strategically attracting both skilled and unskilled workers, we create figurative and literal walls to prevent the very prosperity those immigrants bring.

Is it possible to have too great thinkers? Is it possible to have too many ambitious entrepreneurs? Are we that fearful of competition that we eliminate it before it can occur? It is an odd plea, indeed, to demand that the U.S. embrace its own heritage of melting-pot industry and achievement. By restricting our policies to family reunification, by limiting our access to capital, ambition and brains, we foster a population that stagnates, fundamentally dissatisfied with their lives; and we generate an atmosphere of inertia and fear. By restricting others, we harm ourselves.

As noted, while the United States has been restricting incoming immigrants since 9/11, Canada has more than doubled its numbers, stimulating a much faster recovery from The Great Recession while building a wider and more stable economic future by creating an economic class of immigrants that makes up 55.4% of new permanent residences. Australia has reformed its immigration policy, providing for visa qualification for those making capital investments in real estate, allowing for an influx in population that now positions Australia at the top of global property values; this staggering result comes as the American real estate market continues to suffer.

The European Union, which has been battling a wide range of issues associated with population decline, has begun to seriously compete for immigrants as well. France exemplifies some of the most sensible reforms, allowing adult children of immigrants to naturalize after five years residency with proactive policies which combat discrimination. In this way, France is able to retain more students and young entrepreneurs, as well as unskilled workers, and keep them by offering them the opportunity of a better life.

It's no secret that the United States does not treat its newcomers well — either by policy or public attitude — when we don't actively turn them away; discrimination is an all-too-real condition for immigrants of every color. Current laws promote this close-minded attitude, fostering a climate of fear, hatred and the potential for violence.

Fundamentally, we must join the global competition for brain-power by examining how policy reform has benefited other countries and exemplifying the most useful aspects in our own legislation. In the most literal sense, every day of delay brings losses of untold proportions. By examining the policies of other countries, we can begin to see how we can specify our own criteria for new citizens in order to maximize our attractiveness to skilled workers and thinkers as a country of opportunity.

Canada: Beating U.S. for Foreign Brain Power

As previously described, Canada has the highest percentage population of immigrants among Westernized countries. Canada has been startlingly successful fostering a welcoming environment for newcomers while simultaneously implementing thoughtful policy by specifying a class system that maximizes the productivity of this new population. Canada creates a welcoming, diverse atmosphere for immigrants, tackles issues of discrimination head-on, and utilizes a class structure to carefully categorize the benefits each different immigrant has to offer.[1] In this way, Canada has gained a reputation for being a positive, welcoming and rewarding destination for immigrants, and is the clear leader for persons who might contribute to the brain gain for any country.

Canada divides its new population into classifications, each new citizen falling into one of the following categories:

- Family
- Refugee
- Economic Class
- Skilled Workers
- Business Immigrants.

Each class exemplifies a contribution to Canada's multicultural society, the most significant being the latter three which make up the majority of Canada's incoming population. The largest portion

---

1 Munroe, Eagles; "Canadian-American Relations in a Turbulant Era," *Political Science and Politics*, American Political Science Association, vol. 39 is. 4; October 2006.

of immigrant classification is the Economic category, which made up 55.4% of new permanent residents in 2007. Because of this methodology, the majority of the new immigration population are workers who contribute to Canada's overall economic growth by taking entry-level jobs.[1]

In this area, the United State's most comparable "classification" would be our population of illegal immigrants whom continue to take these jobs for less than minimum wage, inhibiting opportunities for prosperity for themselves and the country in general.

Overall, Canada's immigrant population contributed 70% of the country's net labor force growth in 2007. These numbers signify a win-win situation for both Canada and immigrants looking for a new life in a land thriving with untold opportunity.

The formal immigrant classification structure of Canada bears other benefits as well. Because Canada specifies new residents based on their potential economic contributions, they are also able to track the number of immigrants entering with certain visas, measuring projected growth rates for coming years in categories defined by social, humanitarian, and economic benefits, unlike the United States whose emphasis is mostly on family reunification which has virtually no tracking and limited quantifiable benefits.

By specifying a "Family" classification, Canada is able to put limitations on immigrants who become citizens based on family members' eligibility. As of now, the Family sector is compromised of spouses, dependent children and children intended to be adopted, and/or parents and grandparents.

Canada also specifies which non-immediate family members may immigrate: nieces, nephews, aunts, uncles, and grandchildren may immigrant if they are orphaned, below the age of 18, and single. Canada creates allowances for family members to immigrate through the family class if a sponsor does not have any direct family that meets the aforementioned qualifications. The United States could learn from this model of family reunification, putting more stringent restrictions on who is eligible to immigrate based on their direct relations to a sponsor already living in our country. Current-

1 Munroe, *ibid.*

ly, we allow anyone to join family members already residing in the United States rather than valuing concrete economic contributions over mere reunification.

While this stance may seem callous, it is exactly the opposite. The assertions contained in this book do not advocate *against* family unification but, rather, specify that we must question every priority and its impact on our country and society. To blindly advocate family reunification over every other criterion is irresponsible policy and dangerous practice, to say the least. The policy of family reunification must be intended to benefit *all* families in the United States, not just the ones separated by circumstances of residence.

Canada is also an attractive country to immigrants because it is a leading advocate for human rights in developed countries. Among other issues of concern to immigrants, Canada is one of the few countries to acknowledge same-sex unions nationwide and prides itself on having a multi-cultural array of citizens and subcultures, as opposed to the United States where the overriding attitude is the direction to conform to Americanized cultural ideas and trends. Canada's Refugee classification provides a potential safe haven to those persons facing persecution in other countries. While these qualities, at first glance, do not seem to contribute to a tangible benefit for the growth of Canada, they do foster attitudes of acceptance and goodwill, making Canada more attractive in comparison to the United States, a country which is earning a reputation for racist and xenophobic behaviors.

After 9/11, Canada's policy for relatively straightforward and less painless immigration created a rift in relations with the United States. Previously the U.S. competed directly with Canada for skilled and unskilled workers, but terrorist attacks promoted an attitude of fear and racism toward immigrants. While the U.S. was once known as the Land of Opportunity, we have compromised long-standing ideals of freedom and equality in favor of attitudes of exclusivity, stances which have contributed both to our economic decline and further strained relationships with allies and enemies alike.

While critics say that the terrorists who committed the attacks on the Twin Towers entered the United States and lived here for years under student visas, the draconian new policies have restricted accessibility for all immigrants, particularly refugees, while Canada has continued to embrace its growing immigrant work force and reap the benefits of that thriving population.

The Canada/U.S. Safe Third Country Agreement, implemented out of post-9/11 fear of the U.S. northern border being a weak security area, literally hands over a significant population of immigrants to our northern neighbors by making immigration from Canada to the United States much more difficult.[1] While in the past the U.S. benefited from relatively lax border laws that allowed us to utilize Canada's already carefully selected immigration population, U.S. policy has shut the door entirely, forcing the potential refugee population toward our northern neighbors. This policy has not only decreased U.S. attractiveness as an immigration destination but created a negative public perception towards America among Canadians themselves.

These conditions can be remedied by showing Canadians the U.S. can heal from past bad experiences and will work to improve international relationships, creating reform that allows us to reenter the competition for economic growth and social progress.

Australia: Down Under Rises

While Canada is worthy of examination and comparison to U.S. immigration policy, due to its close proximity and glaring success as a global competitor for a well-defined immigrant work force, other countries' immigration reforms also outstrip the U.S. in the competition for labor, capital and brain power.

Following Canada, Australia is also similar to the United States in terms of its formation, growth and history as a Westernized first-world country. While the U.S. actively seeks to repel immigrants from nearby countries, Australia works to attract those potential residents, drawing significantly from the professional population

---

1 Australian Associated Press (http://news.smh.com.au/breaking-news-national/nsw-migrant-magnet-despite-fall-survey-20110120-19xa7.html).

of China and India,[1] two countries that have gained a reputation for high standards in education and entrepreneurship. Australia already has the advantage of proximity to these countries but the U.S. still needs to enter into competition for these skilled minds.

Australia was virtually forced to reform progressive immigration as a solution to its own brain drain as an increasing number of its natural-born citizens accept jobs overseas, creating an environment of "brain circulation."[2] In 2009, 1 million Australians (10% of the working population) worked overseas, while 700,000 immigrants entered the resident workforce, with an additional 170,000 workers waiting for skilled visa approval. The need for reform to acquire workers and stimulate economic growth was obvious.

In short, Australia is competing for skilled workers in order to compensate for a loss in population while America ignores this need and works against the opportunities.[3] Australia is benefiting from its circulating population, stimulating one of the fastest recoveries from global recession while building long term economic prosperity. The United States continues to lag while wondering what went wrong, despite the evidence all around.

Countries in Europe that have experienced sharp population decline for decades are taking cues from Australia's brain circulation. France is embracing this trend, admitting immigrants in categories similar to Canada's formal classification system.[4] While countries in Europe generally have lower immigration rates and are less enthusiastic towards immigration, recent declines in population necessitate competition for growth in these countries. The prevailing sentiment is to take action or risk worse economic and social problems.

---

1 Carlisle, Wendy. http://www.abc.net.au/rn/backgroundbriefing/stories/2006/1662023.htm#transcript

2 http://www.migrationexpert.com/australia/visa/australian_immigration_news/2011/jan/0/408/australia_needs_to_speed_up_skilled_work_visa_application
   Still, Judith; "France and the Paradigm of Hospitality" http://web.ebscohost.com.emils.lib.colum.edu/ehost/pdfviewer/pdfviewer?hid=21&sid=ffdfc402-a780-46e5-8137-c6 72cb9e526b%40sessionmgr13&vid=12

3 Still, Judith;"France and the Paradigm of Hospitality"http://web.ebscohost.com.emils.lib.colum.edu/ehost/pdfviewer/pdfviewer?hid=21&sid=ffdfc402-a780-46e5-8137-c6 72cb9e526b%40sessionmgr13&vid=12

4 Hainmuller, Jens; "Educated Preferences: Explaining Attitudes toward Immigration in Europe" http://www.jstor.org.emils.lib.colum.edu/stable/4498150

European countries generally have not adapted the melting pot ideals once embraced in the United States, and currently thriving in Canada and Australia, but there is a strong correlation between Europe's overall emphasis on higher education and widespread attitudes of tolerance towards immigrants and children of immigrants.[1] European countries are quickly adopting incentives to attract new populations, and are even beginning to compete for U.S. brains, capital and manpower.

In summary, there is a fierce global competition taking place that the United States has been actively choosing to ignore in recent years. While other Westernized countries have stepped up incentives for immigrant brains, muscle and money, the United States has done the exact opposite. The U.S. must shift emphasis from family reunification to taking part in a global campaign for brain power and labor force, making up for lost time and returning to the true Land of Opportunity. If we intend to continue to be the Land of the Free, we must also be Home of the Brave, and Resourceful.

---

1 Id. Hainmuller

3. The Department of Homeland Security:

Dealing with the Bureaucracy

There is probably no other agency in the federal government more maligned or criticized than the Department of Homeland Security (DHS) (reorganized from the Immigration & Naturalization Service in 2003). Comprised largely of ex-military and former law enforcement personnel, the Department has a reputation for playing hardball and lacking compassion. I recall vividly a former co-counsel of mine, James K. Robinson, the former U.S. Attorney in Detroit, telling me that there are two agencies of the federal government that don't negotiate. One is the Federal Bureau of Prisons. The other is the Immigration & Naturalization Service!

To be sure, there are lots of fine people in the Department of Homeland Security, trying to do a good job every day, but they find themselves overwhelmed by an unrealistic caseload, lack of resources and a hopeless bureaucracy. There were many officers in the Department that made me furious by what I considered to be constant overreach with their groundless and arbitrary decisions, yet at the same time, oddly enough, I felt some sympathy for them. They were trying to do their best, but were trapped in a twisted system. In many respects, they faced a similar plight to the daily life of an immigration lawyer — dealing with too many difficult people, problems with language and communication, and a lack of adequate resources to do a thorough job.

My most vivid experience with the INS was the time we had just scored a major victory in federal court, where the court ordered INS to issue 92 visas to British automotive design engineers whose visa applications had been wrongly denied. We were summoned to a meeting at the INS District office to discuss the implementation of the court's order and the procedure for issuance of the visas. I will never forget the atmosphere in that room. It felt like the Titanic crashing into the iceberg. The District Director and Assistant Director of INS sat at one end of the table, stoic and steely eyed. I sat at the other end of the table with my co-counsel, the former U.S. attorney in town. Thank goodness he was there beside me; after all, he used to be one of them! I am sure if they had it their way, they would have preferred to strangle me. It's not every day that someone knocks the almighty U.S. government off their pedestal. They were used to being omnipotent and untouchable, with absolute power, not eating humble pie.

The Immigration & Naturalization Service was established in 1933 and remained intact until it was dissolved in 2003, when it was reorganized as the Department of Homeland Security. Its origins, however, date back to the 19th century. The Immigration Act of 1891 established an Office of the Superintendent of Immigration within the Treasury Department. Prior to 1891, immigration was regulated by the States; however, in 1875 the Supreme Court ruled that immigration was a federal responsibility. Hence, the first federal agency was created 6 years later.

The Homeland Security Act (HSA), which created the Department of Homeland Security, divided the immigration function — which had previously been the sole province of the former INS — into three agencies: (1) U.S. Customs and Border Protection (CBP), (2) U.S. Immigration and Customs Enforcement (ICE) which handles interior enforcement such as workplace raids and deportation, and (3) United States Citizenship and Immigration Services (US-

CIS) which has responsibility for adjudicating visa applications and petitions.

Subverting the Rule of Law

With all of the talk about securing our borders, illegal immigration, border enforcement, the constitutionality of the Arizona immigration law and the like, one would have thought the Department of Homeland Security would have welcomed with open arms and indeed facilitated the visa applications of those who sought to gain entry to the U.S. legally? Nothing could be farther from the truth or reality of that statement. In fact, since 2001, the Department, via a series of policy memos, guidelines, published and unpublished regulations, has been engaged in an unrelenting suffocation and outright destruction of the legal immigration process.

How has this transpired, you ask, in a country which is supposed to adhere to the rule of law? The problem lies first with the Congress who has the responsibility for enacting our immigration laws. Virtually every immigration enactment ever conceived by the Congress contains a series of key words and criteria, the interpretation and implementation of which has been delegated to the agency to determine. So while the Congress enacts the immigration laws, the Department of Homeland Security is left with the job of defining key words and phrases and promulgating policies and regulations which will determine the standards and levels of evidence one must meet in order to be a successful visa applicant.

Perhaps the first thing practitioners in the immigration field began to notice a few years after 2001 was the Department's increased issuance of something called a Request for Evidence (RFE). These RFEs, as they are known , were often lengthy requests (often 10 pages or more) for further evidence, support and proof of one's eligibility for the sought after visa. Often obscure and unintelligible, these requests have in many instances been impossible to answer or at the very least they imposed substantial burdens on employers and their attorneys to proffer forms of proof which either do not exist or cannot be obtained. With respect to legality, RFEs often contain request for proof which does not appear in any of the immigration statutes enacted by the Congress, nor could a reasonable man infer that such requests could be a logical extension of the law the Congress enacted or that they represented anything close to the intent of the Congress in enacting such legislation. Applicants received RFEs which asked employers to prove that they were an actual company doing business, notwithstanding the fact they were a public company with a listing on the NYSE or the NASDAQ!

In the area of Intra-Company Transferee visas, so-called L-1 visas, the Department's assaults have been no less than brutal. The L-1B Intra-company Transferee classification, together with the L-1A for executives and managers, has existed since 1970. The L1-B allows a U.S. company to transfer employees from the employ of the foreign subsidiary, providing that it is under at least 50% owned or controlled by the U.S. company. To be eligible for the L-1B, applicants must have worked for at least one year for the foreign entity in a job involving "specialized knowledge" and must be seeking work in a like capacity with the U.S. company. The definition of "specialized knowledge" has been at the epicenter of the Department's assault. Since the passage of the Immigration Act of 1990, "specialized knowledge" has required either "special knowledge possessed by the applicant" of the company's products, services, research or equipment or "an advanced knowledge or expertise in the organization's processes and procedures."

Starting in 2008, the USCIS published a non-precedent decision which moved the goalposts substantially from the above criteria, even though there had been no new legislative enactments since the Immigration Act of 1990. The data for employees with specialized knowledge shows a steep rise in denials and requests for evidence beginning in 2008. The denial rate for L-1B petitions more than tripled in 2008 and is now at nearly quadruple the pre-2008 rate, at 27 per cent in 2011. Denial rates rose 75 percent over five years, from 8 percent in 2007 to 14 percent in 2011. The RFE rate is even more telling. From 2005 to 2011, the rate soared from percent to 63 percent.

In the L1-A category, for managers and executives, the RFE rate rose from 10 percent in 2005 to 51 percent in 2011.[1]

But the Department hasn't stopped there. The H1-B category, intended and used by high tech behemoths such as Microsoft, Cisco and Googles of the world, has also come under assault. Once again, with no new legislation from the Congress, the Department issued the so-called "Neufeld memo" in 2008 which sought to unilaterally redefine the employer–employee relationship for workers located at third party client sites. Implementation of the new rogue policy began immediately, just a few days after its issuance, at various U.S. airports where incoming H1-B visa holders were held for interrogation — with some being subjected to expedited removal. The denial rate for H1-B petitions increased 11 percent in 2007 to 17 percent in 2011, with better than 25 percent of filings generating RFEs in 2011.

What sayeth the courts and the judicial process to all of this? The starting point in this inquiry is the longstanding tradition of judicial deference to administrative agencies. Simply put, courts are reluctant to get involved in or to overrule decisions made by the agencies, on the theory that Congress delegated the authority to agencies to promulgate rules and regulations and that the courts should intervene only in limited instances. Congress even tried to strip the courts of jurisdiction to review immigration decisions, and succeeded when they enacted the Antiterrorism and Effective Death Penalty Act of 1996 (IIRIRA).

In 2010, the U.S. Court of Appeals in the Ninth Circuit addressed the matter of the Department's inventing, interjecting and superimposing policies, rules and regulations wholly absent from the laws the Congress enacted. The *Kazarian*[2] case involved an application for a permanent visa under the extraordinary ability category. In that case, the Department sought to impose requirements beyond those which were published in their own regulations. The court found that in two of the required categories, the agency had superimposed requirements that did not exist in their regulations and overruled

---

1 Cyrus D. Mehta, "*Stop the Assault on Employment Immigration to the USA,*" *The Insightful Immigration Blog,* March 2, 2012
2 *Kazarian v. USCIS,* 596 F.3d., 1115 (9th. Cir. 2010).

the Department's finding in those two specific categories. At the end of the day, however, Kazarian lost his case because the court determined he had not met the requirements of the four required categories of qualification.

While the *Karzarian* case is a welcome relief to the legal assault on legal immigration, if past practice is any indication, it is likely to have no or little effect on the DHS. First, the decision, even if the plaintiff had prevailed, would only have applied to him. While the "precedent" is comforting, if one can call it that, it is doubtful that the case will change anything in the way the Department adjudicates applications. The reality is that 99% of applicants do not have the resources or the tools to get to federal court to have their applications reviewed, and the Department knows this. So, while they may be a sporadic victory along the way, it's hard to view the decision as a breakthrough.

Changing the Culture

In 2001, President George Bush nominated James Ziglar as the new Commissioner of the INS. In his July 2001 confirmation hearings, Ziglar advised "overhauling" the INS, and affirmed the goals that President Bush had outlined at Ellis Island:

> "If I am confirmed for this position, my primary goal will be to insure that every person who comes into contact with the Immigration and Naturalization Service, regardless of their citizenship, the circumstances of their birth or any other distinguishing characteristic, and regardless of the circumstances under which they find themselves within the ambit of the INS, will be treated with respect and dignity, and without any hint of bias or discrimination.
>
> "I will encourage the employment of common sense, compassion and good judgment in the decision-making process at every level, particularly those areas where the INS has wide discretion. I believe that the vast majority of INS employees today are exercising that good judgment. But there are instances where common sense has not prevailed or discretion has been abused. We will not tolerate such actions or conduct.... I am convinced that an overhaul is needed."[1]

---

1 Senate Confirmation Hearings of James Ziglar, July 18, 2001

Prior to being nominated, Mr. Ziglar was Sergeant at Arms and Doorkeeper of the United States Senate. He was an accomplished lawyer holding partner positions at numerous NYC law firms as well as an investment banker with Paine Webber among others. Senators on both sides of the aisle praised Ziglar. He was confirmed by unanimous consent.

James Ziglar resigned his post on November 30, 2002, just 16 months after assuming the position on August 6, 2001. "It is no surprise that James Ziglar has decided to leave his post as Commissioner of the INS. The Agency was a disaster before he arrived and did not improve after." so reported the Brookings Institutions in July of 2012.

James Ziglar was the last Commissioner of the INS. Shortly after his resignation, the INS was reorganized into the Department of Homeland Security in which the U.S. Citizenship and Immigration Services Department was created to assume the visa application and adjudication functions formerly performed by the INS.

Dr. Emilio T. Gonzalez, a Cuban-born Ph.D. from the Univ. of Miami and 26-year army veteran who had spent most of his professional career in foreign affairs and international security policy, became the first Director of the newly formed USCIS in December 2005. Dr. Gonzalez lasted just over two years, resigning on March 13, 2008. There were several reports that Gonzalez' inability to improve the USCIS backlogs led to his demise. But Debbie Schlussel, lawyer, radio talk show host and conservative political commentator, went even further:

> "Emilio T. Gonzalez, the incompetent head of U.S. Citizenship and Immigration Services — the agency that spends less than 6 minutes reviewing each request for green cards and citizenship — has resigned.

> "Gonzalez, as you'll recall, is the guy who gave himself an award he created for "Outstanding American by Choice" (an award that illegally discriminates against Americans on the basis of national original because if you are a natural born citizen, you couldn't receive it). He's also the guy who sicced federal agents on his former Director of Security, Michael Maxwell, for daring to speak out against lax scrutiny of aliens seeking entry to and citizenship in our country.

"At least one USCIS employee whom I respect disagrees with me, though, in applauding Gonzalez's departure. The employee points out that Bush will simply nominate another incompetent to fill the job for the remainder of his last year in office, and that Gonzalez was a nice, if ignorant person (ignorance is bliss). The employee tells me that it's better to have a nice incompetent than a creepy, vindictive incompetent (like Julie L. Myers and John Torres at ICE) running the agency. Because, after all, the USCIS employee tells me, 'The whole entity is terminal and beyond repair.'

"Yup, that's how bad things are. Good employees have given up on the system working. They're at the point where they will merely settle for a nice guy idiot over a bad guy idiot.

"Good luck, America."[1]

The foregoing comments by Debbie Schlussel probably represent an overly harsh view of the Department. The reality is that the DHS does process millions of applications a year, and although a few fee receipts and files may get lost, and many cases take far too long to get processed, the system does function — not perfectly, but nevertheless it functions. And one should not underestimate the enormous task of processing millions of applications a year with limited resources.

Comments about past heads of the Department being chastised for allowing the agency to spend just 6 minutes reviewing an application frankly miss the point. Commissioner Gonzalez was attempting to speed up the review of applications and clear the huge backlogs in processing for which he was criticized. What really counts is not whether an adjudicator spends 6 minutes or 6 hours in the review process. Rather, what's important is that every review and decision adheres to the rule of law; and that the Department cease dreaming up policy memos, inventing law and adopting regulations that are questionable interpretations of the statutes Congress enacted. Until that happens, it doesn't matter what laws the Congress passes; legal immigration has a problem.

---

1 Id, Debbie Schlussel, *"Adios, Emilio: Incompetent Who Headed Immigration Agency Resigns,"* March 13, 2008.

4. The Rise of the Administrative State

The rise of administrative bodies probably has been the most significant legal trend of the last century and perhaps more values today are affected by their decisions than by those of all the courts, review of administrative decisions apart.... They have become a veritable fourth branch of the Government, which has deranged our three-branch legal theories much as the concept of a fourth dimension unsettles our three-dimensional thinking.
— *FTC v. Ruberoid Co., 343 U.S. 470, 487 (1952).*

Part I — The Context

Most of the real lawmaking in modern-day America occurs in bureaucracies. The Federal Register alone comprises some 70,000 pages annually. Any attempt at congressional oversight of these bureaucracies is impossible; the sheer size of the so-called Administrative State[1] is as incomprehensible as it is unconstitutional. Scholars will tell you that we no longer live under the Constitution and its three branches of government. Rather, we live under the administrative law of an Administrative State, a de facto fourth branch of government. This fourth branch of government is one that James

---

1 J. Freedman, *Crisis and Legitimacy* 6 (1978).

Madison in *The Federalist* would have deemed "the very essence of tyranny."[1]

The general public has not paid much attention to the rise of the administrative state because "the connection between politics and administration arouses remarkably little interest in the United States. The presidency is considered more glamorous, Congress more intriguing, elections more exciting, and interest groups more troublesome."[2]

The genesis of the problem rests with the U.S. Constitution itself, which provides little guidance regarding the line between making laws and executing them:

> When the Constitution assigned the legislative power to the Congress and the executive power to the president, it offered no abstract definition of either and demarked no precise boundary between them. Authorizing the government to do things is clearly legislative; doing them is plainly executive, but in between is a vast borderland: how the executive shall go about executing the law.[3]

The Constitution does not mention agencies at all. Professor Erwin Chemerinsky has noted that "in fact, in many ways [agencies] are in tension with basic constitutional principles."[4] Agencies can make rules that have the force of law and many scholars argue that this conflicts with the basic separation-of-powers notion "that Congress alone possesses the federal legislative power."[5]

With no clear definition or direction from the Constitution as to the propriety of this transfer of power from Congress to the administrative branch, scholars have produced mountains of literature debating the constitutionality of this delegation.[6] This argument is premised upon the non-delegation doctrine, enunciating "the principle that Congress may not delegate its legislative power

1 A. M. Gulas, *The American Administrative State: The New Leviathan*, 28 DUQ. L. REV. 489, 490 (1990).
2 Hugh Heclo, *Issue Networks and the Executive Establishment*, in THE NEW AMERICAN POLITICAL SYSTEM, (Anthony King, ed., Amer. Enterprise Institute) (1978).
3 James Sunquist, *The Decline and Resurgence of Congress* 37 (1981).
4 Erwin Chemerinsky, *Constitutional Law: Principles and Policies* 319 (2d ed. 2002).
5 *Id.*
6 Louis Fisher, *Constitutional Conflicts Between Congress and the President* (4th ed. 1997).

to administrative agencies."[1] Professor Kagan explains the argument in a nutshell as follows:

> Basic separation of powers doctrine maintains that Congress must authorize presidential exercises of essentially lawmaking functions. In directing agency officials as to the use of their delegated discretion, the President engages in such functions, but without the requisite congressional authority. Congress indeed has delegated discretionary power, but only to specified executive branch officials; by assuming responsibility for this power, the President thus exceeds the appropriate bounds of his office. This argument underlies the conventional, though never adjudicated, view that the President lacks directive authority over administrative officials.[2]

Professor Kagan's explanation can be reduced to a more basic form: Only Congress can enact a law. However, the responsibility for interpretation and implementation of that law is vested in the executive branch. Because of the president's increasing influence over the direction and control of agency actions, agencies often promulgate regulations and policies to be consistent with the president's agenda, which may not be consistent with the legislation enacted by Congress.

Individuals unhappy with an agency's rules and regulations may in some instances have the right to challenge the agency in federal court. However, because of judicial deference to administrative agency action, courts often decline to intervene and overrule the agency.[3] Thus, despite sound constitutional principles for maintaining Congress's legislative function, it often appears futile to challenge administrative actions for alleged violations of the non-delegation doctrine. At one time, the Supreme Court showed a willingness to strike down federal laws as invalid delegations of legislative power; however, the last time it did so was in 1935.[4] The

---

1 Chemerinsky, *supra* note 6, at 319-20.

2 Elena Kagan, *Presidential Administration*, 114 HARV. L. REV. 2245, 2319-20 (2001).

3 Donald S. Dobkin, "The Diminishing Prospects for Legal Immigration: Clinton through Bush," 19 St. Thomas L. Rev. 329 (2006).

4 See Chemerinsky *supra* note 6, at 320 (citing *Panama Refining Co. v. Ryan*, 293 U.S. 388 (1935); *Schecter Poultry Corp. v. United States*, 295 U.S. 495 (1935)). The non-delegation doctrine was almost revived in recent years when the U.S. Court of Appeals for the D.C. Circuit found an impermissible delegation of legislative powers in

inevitable result of the current state of affairs is that Congressio-nally-enacted laws are either ignored or so modified by the execu-tive's stranglehold on administrative agencies that they often are implemented and enforced in ways that are contrary to the will of the Congress.[1] This administrative domination is only exacerbated when courts then abdicate their responsibility to provide effective judicial review to reinforce constitutional principles.

Part II(A) — The Rise of Presidential Administration and Executive Power

Professor Kagan has described the evolution of the administra-tive process as follows:

> At the dawn of the regulatory state, Congress controlled admin-istrative action by legislating precisely and clearly; agencies, far from exercising any worrisome discretion, functioned as mere "transmission belts[s]" to carry out legislative directives. But as the Administrative State grew and then the New Deal emerged, Congress routinely resorted to broad delegations, giving sub-stantial, unfettered discretion to agency officials. With this change came a justifying theory, which stressed the need for professional administrators, applying a neutral and impartial expertise, to set themselves the direction and terms of regula-tion. As the years passed, however, faith in the objectivity of these administrators eroded, and in consequence, an array of interest groups received enhanced opportunities to influence agency conduct.[2]

For many years, political scientists and other observers of government generally agreed that once Congress made these del-egations, it had affirmatively chosen not to exercise any effective control over administrative policymaking. Adherents to this view pointed to the rarity of any visible use by Congress of its remaining levers of control — its ability it block statutory mandates, reverse

---

the Clean Air Act's delegation to the EPA to promulgate certain air quality regu-lations. The Supreme Court granted certiorari and unanimously reversed on this point, holding that the Clean Air Act did not violate the non-delegation doc-trine. *Amer. Trucking Ass'ns, Inc.*, 531 U.S. 457, 474 (2001). Because the Clean Air Act contained "intelligible principles" to guide the agency, nothing more was needed to avoid violating the non- delegation doctrine. *Id.*

1 *Id.*
2 Kagan, *supra* note 10, at 2253.

administrative decisions, cut agency budgets, block presidential nominees, or even conduct serious oversight hearings.[1]

Presidential control over administrative agencies took a giant step forward in the Reagan administration through the expanded use of executive orders. Exec. Order No. 12,291, 46 Fed. Reg. 13193 (Feb. 17, 1981), issued during Reagan's first month in office, required executive agencies to submit to the Office of Management and Budget (OMB) for pre-publication any proposed major rule, accompanied by a "regulatory impact analysis" of the rule, including a cost-benefit comparison. This Order effectively transferred substantive control over rule making to the OMB and by extension, to the executive branch.[2]

Furthermore, the executive branch no longer even needs to wait for Congress to authorize the creation of an agency: "Using executive orders, department orders, and reorganization plans, presidents have unilaterally created a majority of the administrative agencies listed in the *United States Government Manual*."[3] This is a large aberration from the traditional view whereby Congress vests discretion for agency decisions in an agency head, rather than in the President. As Professor Thomas Sargentich has noted, "[i]f Congress had wanted the President to have controlling authority, it could have so provided."[4] When the executive branch actively creates its own agencies, the President is all the more likely to have the ability to exercise controlling authority.

New initiatives introduced in the Clinton administration raised the ante substantially. Faced with a distinctly hostile and partisan Republican Congress, Clinton seized the opportunity to tighten his control over the agencies in order to accomplish by executive order what he could not achieve legislatively. The Administrative

---

1 Lawrence C. Dodd & Richard L. Schott, *Congress and the Administrative State* (1979); *see also infra* Part II(b).

2 Kenneth Mayer, *With the Stoke of a Pen: Executive Orders And Presidential Power* (2001).

3 William J. Howell, *Power Without Persuasion: The Politics of Direct Presidential Action* (2003).

4 Thomas O. Sargentich, *The Emphasis on the Presidency in U.S. Public Law: An Essay Critiquing Presidential Administration*, 59 ADMIN. L. REV. 1, 10 (2007); *see also id.* at 24 ("On its face, a statutory delegation to an agency head indicates that the agency head is to be the decision-maker.").

State expanded significantly during Clinton's eight years in office, forcing him the center of the regulatory landscape.[1] Professor Sargentich has summarized Clinton's actions during these years as giving regulatory oversight "a new substantive turn."[2] The changes included "formal directives to executive branch officials regarding the exercise of their statutory discretion."[3]

In this way, Clinton was able to perfect the art of "go-alone governing."[4] For instance, when his 1993 health care initiative went nowhere, Clinton subsequently managed to "issue directives that established a patient's bill of rights for federal employees, reformed health care programs' appeals processes, and set new penalties for companies that denied health coverage to the poor, and people with pre-existing medical conditions."[5] With the expanded use of executive orders, Clinton was able to achieve with a pen what he could not achieve on the Hill. Clinton's use of directives "effectively placed him in the position of a department head."[6] In this position, the President was able to pass wide-sweeping reforms.

Because an agency's actions often receive far less media attention than the actions of the President, the general public is often unaware of political decisions being made at the agency level. This lack of accountability in general makes it easier to pursue a political agenda at the agency level.[7]

President George W. Bush has also used the inattention to agency action to pursue some of the more unpopular aspects of his political agenda to avoid direct accountability. For example, rather than openly challenging environmental protections, President Bush has used agencies to help him pursue his anti-environmental agen-

---

1 Kagan, *supra* note 10, at 2281.

2 Sargentich, *supra* note 16, at 14.

3 Kagan, *supra* note 10, at 2293.

4 William J. Howell, "Unilateral Powers: A Brief Overview," 35 *PRESIDENTIAL STUD. Q.* 417, 418 (2005 (citations omitted).

5 *Id.*

6 Thomas O. Sargentich, *supra* note 16 at 13 (citing Kagan, *supra* note 10, at 2306).

7 *Cf.* Robert R.M. Verchick, *Toward Normative Rules for Agency Interpretation: Defining Jurisdiction Under the Clean Water Act*, 55 ALA. L. REV. 845, 858 (2004) ("[Professor] Kagan acknowledges the possibility that a President might use his or her power to inappropriately cloud issues and avoid accountability, but she grossly underestimates the danger.").

da to ensure the "systematic dismantling of various environmental regulations."[1]

The White House's tightening of control via executive orders had its origins in the alteration of the context of presidential leadership during the 1960s and 1970s:

> In an era of growing budget deficits, divided government, a more open political process, and a general loss of public faith in "big government," presidents beginning with Richard Nixon no longer saw unalloyed benefits in relying on "neutral" staff agencies. Instead, they sought greater political responsiveness. This meant relying more heavily on aides within the White House Office, and appointing political loyalists to exercise top- down control of the other Executive Office of the President (EOP) agencies.[2]

Table 1 illustrates the magnitude of the EOP, which by 2004 had reached 1,731 staffers ranging from everything to Homeland Security Staff, OMB, CEA, and other agencies:

TABLE 1: The Executive Office of the President

Agency	Employees	Year Est.
White House Office	406	1939
(Includes Homeland Security Staff)	(2001)	
Office of the Vice President	24	1972
Office of Management and Budget	521	1921
Office of Administration	212	1977
Council of Economic Advisers	28	1946
Council on Environmental Quality	22	1969
Office of Policy Development	32	1970

---

1 Sargentich, *supra* note 16, at 34 n.147 (2007) (citing Charles Tiefer, *Veering Right: How the Bush Administration Subverts the Law for Conservative Causes* 121-23 (2004)); *see also* TIEFER, *supra*, at 104 ("After he rolled back President Clinton's popular legacy initiatives, [President Bush] mounted from November 2002 through 2004 an anti- environmental campaign, including secrecy aspects . . . .").

2 Matthew Dickson, *The Executive Office of the President: The Paradox of Politicization, in* THE EXECUTIVE BRANCH 135,137 (Joel D. Aberbach & Mark A. Peterson eds., 2005).

(Includes National Economic Council)	(1993)	
(Includes Domestic Council)	(1993)	
Executive Residence at the White House	90	
National Security Council	54	1947
Office of National Drug Control Policy	102	1988
Office of Science and Technology Policy	28	1976
Office of the U.S. Trade Representative	212	1963
Total EOP Employment (as of May 2004)	1,731	
SOURCE: *Office of Personnel Management*1		

During this same time period, "presidents have increased the number of political appointees at the upper levels of the non-White House EOP agencies, and brought the agencies more tightly under White House staff control."[1] The appointment process has allowed presidents to use agencies as a means for major — and often unpopular — policy changes. For instance, President Reagan made "a series of fox-in-the-chicken-coop appointments to undermine public interest regulation," notably of his infamous anti-environment environment interior secretary, James Watt.[2] Many commentators have noted that the current Bush Administration has made similar appointments.[3]

These types of appointments make it difficult for agencies to exhibit expertise and to execute the law in an impartial manner. As a result, we are left with "a more thoroughly politicized, White House-dominated EOP, but one that is short on institutional memory, administrative expertise, and organizational continuity."[4]

---

1 *Id.*
2 Tiefer, *supra* note 24, at 106.
3 E.g., James Gerstenzang, "Bush's Choice for Consumer Post Criticized," *Los Angeles Times*, Mar. 2, 2007, at 21.
4 Tiefer, *supra* note 24, at 106.

The rise in the presidentially-led Administrative States merely reflects the growing use — and creation — of unilateral powers by the President:

> To pursue a unilateral strategy, of course, presidents must be able to justify their actions on some blend of statutory, treaty or constitutional powers; and when they cannot, their only recourse is legislation. But given the ambiguity of Article II powers and the massive corpus of law that presidents can draw upon . . . the appeal of unilateral powers is readily apparent.[1]

Although some would argue that a unilateral executive branch is justified based on the majoritarian "mandate" produced by a presidential election, it is difficult to take this notion very seriously when "a President can be elected without obtaining a majority of the popular vote — as in the cases of President Clinton in 1992 and 1996 and President George W. Bush in 2000."[2] Indeed, in the 2000 election, the winning candidate did not even garner a plurality of the popular vote.[3] Furthermore, presidential elections often center on issues like national security, which are far removed from the everyday decisions of administrative agencies.[4]

The situation is only likely to worsen. In the early days of President George W. Bush's administration, Professor Kagan predicted that President Bush would continue Clinton's "expansion of presidential administration."[5]

Professor Sargentich has noted that this prediction has undoubtedly "come to pass," as exemplified by recent executive branch acts such as the OMB's far-reaching and controversial Peer Review Bulletin, which guides agency decisions.[6]

Part II (B) — The Lack of Congressional Oversight

Congress has vast powers to oversee the actions of federal agencies and the policies they implement:

---

1 Howell, *supra note 20*, at 28.
2 Sargentich, *supra note 16*, at 28.
3 *See* Kagan, *supra note 10*, at 2334.
4 Sargentich, *supra note 16*, at 28.
5 Kagan, *supra note 10*, at 2319.
6 Sargentich, *supra note 16*, at 13 n. 48.

Although the Constitution grants no formal, express authority to oversee or investigate the executive or program administration, oversight is implied in Congress's impressive array of enumerated powers. (Article 1, Sec. 8 and Article II, Secs. 2 and 4). . . . Reinforcing these powers is Congress' broad authority "to make all laws which shall be necessary and proper for carrying into execution the foregoing powers, and all other powers vested by the Constitution in the Government of the United States, or in any Department or Officer thereof."[1]

The standing committee system provides the most obvious means for exercising congressional oversight.[2] However, historically, oversight has occurred in many other contexts, including "authorization, appropriations, and legislative hearings by standing committees; specialized investigations by select committees; and reviews and studies by congressional support agencies and staff."[3]

The Necessary and Proper Clause has been interpreted to allow Congress "to enact laws that mandate oversight by its committees, grant relevant authority to itself and its support agencies, and impose specific obligations on the executive to report to or consult with Congress, and even seek its approval for specific actions."[4] Several significant statutes also grant broad oversight mandates to Congress:

> The Legislative Reorganization Act of 1946 (P.L. 79-601), for the first time, explicitly called for "legislative oversight" in public law. It directed House and Senate standing committees "to exercise continuous watchfulness" over programs and agencies under their jurisdiction; authorized professional staff for them; and enhanced the powers of the Comptroller General, the head of Congress's investigative and audit arm, the General Accounting Office (GAO). The Legislative Reorganization Act of 1970 (P.L. 91-510) authorized each standing committee to "review and study, on a continuing basis, the application, administration and execution of laws" under its jurisdiction.[5]

---

1 Frederick M. Kaiser, *CONGRESSIONAL OVERSIGHT* 3 (Cong. Research Serv., CRS Report for Congress No. 97-936 GOV, Oct. 10, 1997), *available* at http://counting-california. cdlib.org/crs/ascii/97-936.

2 *Id.* at 1.

3 *Id.*

4 *Id.* at 3.

5 *Id.*

Political science literature analyzing Congressional oversight takes a normative approach and largely concludes that effective congressional oversight is sorely lacking.[1] However, recent literature contrarily argues that Congress does effectively influence agency decision making within a system of "congressional dominance." These studies have shown large statistical increases in formal methods of legislative oversight.[2]

The power over appropriations is of particular importance because it theoretically allows Congress to punish agencies by constraining their funding.[3] The idea is that "an annual appropriations process puts a premium on agencies demonstrating that Congress gets what it pays for."[4] If Congress is upset with an agency's actions, it has the power to bring enormous pressure to bear on that agency: "Potential sanctions for an agency's failure to fulfill statutory mandates include political embarrassment at congressional hearings, vulnerability to auditing and investigation, the threat of losing appropriations, and even elimination of the agency."[5] Nevertheless, as a practical matter, these apparently vast powers are rarely ever used. Even the authors of the studies that claimed to find "congressional dominance" concede that they were unable to effectively assess the quality of such review.[6]

Literature analyzing congressional oversight utilizes a broad definition of oversight and includes budgetary, fiscal, regulatory review, and other powers. Too little, if any, attention has been focused on oversight of agency rules and regulations — an area where Congress seems to be unwilling to play any sort of significant role.

1 E.g., Martin Shapiro, Who Guards The Guardians? (1988).

2 Kagan, supra note 10, at 2257 (citing JOEL D. ABERBACH, KEEPING A WATCHFUL EYE 14, 34-37 (1990)

3 E.g., Curtis A. Bradley & Eric A. Posner, Presidential Signing Statements and Executive Power,23 CONST. COMMENT. 307, 354 (2006) (noting that Congress' control over appropriations is one of several methods Congress can use "to punish agencies that interpret laws in a manner that diverges too far from Congress's intention").

4 Joan H. Krause, "A Patient-Centered Approach to Health Care Fraud Recovery," 96 J. CRIM. L. & CRIMINOLOGY 579, 597 (2006).

5 J.R. DeShazo & Jody Freeman, Public Agencies as Lobbyists, 105 COLUM. L. REV. 2217, 2235-36 (2005).

6 Joel Aberbach, What's Happened to the Watchful Eye, 29 CONGRESS & PRESIDENCY 3, 14 (2002).

After the 1983 Supreme Court decision, *INS v. Chadha,*[1] it took Congress a decade or more to realize that something had to be done to check the unfettered power of administrative agencies over rule-making and regulations. In *Chadha,* the Supreme Court's invalidation of the legislative veto technique seemed to provide the knock-out blow to congressional clout over agency abuse. Prior to this ruling, "Congress placed legislative veto provisions in nearly 300 statutes, allowing one or both houses . . . to overturn, without the President's approval, an agency's exercise of delegated authority."[2] This legislative veto had been successfully used to nullify many orders, including wrongfully-issued USCIS deportation orders.

In 1996, the Congressional Review Act (CRA)[3] was enacted with a purpose "to set in place a mechanism to keep Congress informed about the rule making activities of federal agencies and to allow for expeditious congressional review, and possible nullification of particular rules."[4] It soon became apparent that there were two major flaws in the CRA. First, there was no Congressional screening device capable of identifying particular rules in need of Congressional examination. Second, there was no expedited joint resolution procedure in the House to run concurrently and complimentary with Senate procedures.[5]

In the decade following the enactment of the CRA, "[a]lmost 42,000 rules were reported to Congress over that period, including 610 major rules, and only one, the Labor Department's ergonomics standard, was disapproved in March 2001."[6] Moreover, "[t]hirty-seven disapproval resolutions, directed at 28 rules, [were] introduced during that period, and only three, including the ergonomics rule, passed the Senate."[7]

---

1 462 U.S. 919 (1983).

2 Kagan, *supra* note 10, at 2257.

3 Contract with America Advancement Act of 1996, Pub. L. No. 104-121, §251, 110 Stat. 847, 868-74 (1996).

4 *Congressional Review Act: Hearing Before the Subcomm. on Commercial and Admin. Law of the H. Comm. On the Judiciary,* 109th Cong. (2006) (Statement of Morton Rosenberg, Specialist in American Public Law, Cong. Research Serv.), 2006 WL 833617.

5 *Id.*

6 *Id.*

7 *Id.*

Part II (C) — Judicial Review and the Disappearing Federal Courts

With the effectiveness of the CRA in serious question, we turn our attention to the courts and their intervention, or lack thereof, in the conduct and rule-making power of the agencies. In the decade after enactment of the CRA, federal appellate courts negated all or parts of sixty rules: a number, while significant in some respects is comparatively miniscule in relation to the number of rules (42,000) issued in the period.

Why have courts been so reluctant to intervene to check agency power? The modern cornerstone of the legal doctrine of judicial deference to administrative agencies was laid out in the 1984 Supreme Court decision of *Chevron, U.S.A. Inc. v. Natural Resources Defense Council.*[1] *Chevron* involved the interpretation of the words "stationary source" in the 1977 Amendments to the Clean Air Act.[2] Justice Stevens, delivering the opinion of the court, developed a two-step process for reviewing an agency's construction of a statute. The first step determines whether a statutory provision is ambiguous, and, if it is, the second step determines whether the agency's interpretation is reasonable and therefore deserving of what is now called "*Chevron* deference" by the courts:

First, as always, is the question whether Congress has directly spoken to the precise question at issue. If the intent of the Congress is clear, that is the end of the matter; for the court, as well as the agency, must give effect to the unambiguously expressed intent of Congress. If, however, the court determines Congress has not directly addressed the precise question at issue, the court does not simply impose its own construction of the statute, as would be necessary in the absence of an administrative interpretation. Rather, if the statute is silent or ambiguous with respect to the specific issue, the question for the court is whether the agency's answer is based on a permissible construction on the statute.[3]

---

1 467 U.S. 837 (1984).
2 *Id.*
3 *Id.* 842-44.

The court further clarified the scope of administrative agency power:

> The power of an administrative agency to administer a congressionally created . . . program necessarily requires the formulation of policy and the making of rules to fill any gap left, implicitly or explicitly, by Congress. . . . Congress has explicitly left a gap for the agency to fill, there is an express delegation of authority to the agency to elucidate a specific provision of the statute by regulation. Such legislative regulations are given controlling weight unless they are arbitrary, capricious, or manifestly contrary to the statute.[1]

In establishing the two-part *Chevron* doctrine, the Court revolutionized administrative law. Although the first step of the *Chevron* analysis allows courts to retain their full powers to interpret the clear language of statutory directives, the second step defers to a reasonable agency interpretation. Some authors have suggested that if *Chevron*'s basic holding is: 'ambiguous statutory provisions should be interpreted by agencies rather than the courts,' then *Chevron* may be seen as a "kind of counter-*Marbury* for the Administrative State."[2] To be sure, the principles of judicial deference to agency interpretations laid out by the Supreme Court in *Chevron* caused profound disruption balance among Congress's law-making powers, an executive agency's rule-making powers, and the judicial branch's interpretive powers.[3] The importance of *Chevron* in judicial review of administrative agencies cannot be understated:

> In a remarkably short period, *Chevron* has become one of the most cited cases on all of American law. As of December 2001, *Chevron* has been cited in federal courts over 7000 times — far more than *Brown v. Board of Education*, *Roe v. Wade*, and *Marbury v. Madison*. In terms of sheer citations, *Chevron* may well qualify as the most influential case in the history of American public law.[4]

---

1 *Id.* (citing *Morton v. Ruiz*, 415 U.S. 199, 231 (1974)).

2 Stephen G. Breyer et al., *ADMINISTRATIVE LAW AND REGULATORY POLICY*, 290 (5th ed. 2002).

3 Breyer et al., *supra* note 59 at 289-90.

4 *Id.* Although the Supreme Court has so far been unwilling to hold that an agency's interpretation is unreasonable (a holding that would likely upset the executive branch and lead to charges of judicial activism), the Court sometimes finds a way to reach the same result under a more aggressive application of step one of

To date, an agency's decision has not been invalidated by the Supreme Court under step two of Chevron (though several Courts of Appeal have done so).[1] As a result, agencies are left with enormous latitude in how they interpret ambiguous statutory provisions. It is an understatement to say that the courts have not been proactive in reviewing and negating agency regulations and rule-making authority.65 *Chevron* simply demonstrates the federal judiciary's indifference to filling their docket with review of agency rules and regulations. What is worse, the Supreme Court's record in this regard has been characterized by some as an abdication of judicial responsibility.[2]

Without a doubt, under the Court's guidance, agencies like US-CIS have little fear in construing statutes and issuing regulations. Generally, agencies can establish binding rules through adjudication, rather than through a formal notice-and-comments or informal rulemaking processes.[3] In the first case following the enactment of the Administrative Procedures Act (APA), the Supreme Court in *NLRB v. Wyman-Gordon Co.*[4] held that agencies could formulate rules either through adjudication or formal rule-making channels and that the ultimate choice between the two lies in the agency's discretion.[5]

Despite the agency's choice between adjudication and formal rule-making, the Supreme Court has generally stressed the importance of consistency in administrative agency adjudications. In *Allentown v. Mack Sales & Service, Inc. v. NLRB*, the Court held that an

---

the *Chevron* analysis. *See* Molot, *supra* note 60 (citing FDA v. Brown & Williamson Tobacco Corp., 529 U.S. 120 (2000); MCI Telecomms. Corp. v. AT&T Co., 512 U.S. 218, 227-29 (1994)) ("[C]ourts sometimes have applied *Chevron* quite aggressively.... Where a court works hard to find statutory clarity at *Chevron* Step I, it ends up not only substituting its judgment for that of the relevant agency, but also fixing statutory meaning for all time and enhancing its power vis-à-vis future courts and future political administrations.").

1 Donald S. Dobkin, *The Diminishing Prospects for Legal Immigration: Clinton through Bush*, 19 *ST. THOMAS L. REV.* 329, 340 (2007).

2 *Id.*

3 394 U.S. 759, 781 (1969).

4 5 U.S.C. 554, (2000).

5 *See NLRB*, 394 U.S. at 781.

---

agency must utilize "reasoned decision-making and consistency in adjudication."[1]

Within the immigration arena, the Supreme Court most recently addressed the scope of agency rule-making power in *INS v. Yang*.[2] The central issue in *Yang* was whether a sudden change in USCIS (INS) policy of disregarding entry fraud in determining eligibility for waivers of deportation was permissible. The Court stated:

> Though the agency's discretion is unfettered at the outset, if it announces and follows — by rule or by settled course of adjudication — a general policy by which its exercise of discretion will be governed, an irrational departure from that policy (as opposed to an avowed alteration of it) could constitute action that must be overturned as "arbitrary, capricious, [or] an abuse of discretion" within the meaning of the Administrative Procedure Act, 5 U.S.C. S. 706(2)(A).[3]

Despite paying considerable lip service to the principle that a sudden change in agency practice could be arbitrary if not properly explained or justified, Justice Scalia, noted that "the INS has not, however, disregarded its general policy here; it has merely taken a narrow view of what constitutes 'entry fraud' under that policy"[4] and the net result was the reversal of the Ninth Circuit's decision that held in favor of Yang.[5]

In the 2001 decision, *United States v. Mead Corp.*,[6] the Supreme Court issued its first major decision since *Chevron* that pertained to judicial deference and administrative agencies. *Mead* appeared to alter *Chevron* by imposing a threshold barrier to agencies seeking a *Chevron* defense. Rather than automatically deferring to the agency when statutory ambiguities exist, agencies seeking to implement a particular statutory provision now qualify for *Chevron* deference only "when it appears that Congress delegated authority to the agency generally to make rules carrying the force of law, and

---

1 *Allentown Mack Sales & Serv., Inc. v. NLRB*, 522 U.S. 359,374 (1998).

2 *INS v. Yueh-Shaio Yang*, 519 U.S. 26, 30 (1997).

3 *Id.*, at 32.

4 *Id.*

5 *Id.*

6 *United States v. Mead Corp.*, 533 U.S. 218 (2001).

[where] the agency interpretation claiming deference was promulgated in the exercise of that authority."[1]

While some authors have heralded *Mead* as a major development in administrative law jurisprudence and a setback to unbridled agency power (even proclaiming it as a reversal of the global presumption of judicial deference established by *Chevron*)[2] its impact has yet to be felt in the immigration arena. Federal courts have largely ignored *Mead* in their review of immigration cases, maintaining their "business as usual" posture.[3] Of the few circuits that have cited *Mead* while reviewing immigration cases, only one court has decided to withhold deference based in part on *Mead*.[4]

Part III — A Case Study: USCIS

The Immigration Act of 1990 (INA)[5] contained a novel and breakthrough provision, which allowed aliens of exceptional ability to receive immigrant visas if doing so would serve the United States' national interest. Specifically, the law provided that persons

---

1 *Id.* at 226-27.

2 Adrian Vermeule, *"Mead in the Trenches,"* 71 GEO. WASH. L. REV. 347, 352 (2003).

3 *See, e.g.,* David S. Rubenstein, *"Putting the Immigration Rule of Lenity in Its Proper Place: A Tool of Last Resort After Chevron,"* 59 ADMIN. L. REV. 479, 480 (2007) ("The Supreme Court has historically deferred to the political branches' policy decisions in immigration matters."). *But see* Brian G. Slocum, *Courts vs. the Political Branches: Immigration "Reform" and the Battle for the Future of Immigration Law,* 5 GEORGETOWN J.L. & PUB. POL'Y 509, 511-12 (2007) ("While it is partially accurate, the standard theory of extreme judicial deference to the political branches in immigration matters is typically overstated. The standard account fails to recognize the judiciary's increasing inclination to promote its own version of desirable public values in limited, but extremely important, areas of immigration law. In contrast to the values promoted by Congress and the executive branch through their reforms, the judiciary has, through various methods, pursued a more pro-immigrant set of values. The judiciary's decisions have, for the most part, been made through the (often aggressive) application of mainstream principles of law and statutory interpretation . . . ."). Although Professor Slocum makes a forceful argument that the judicial branch has played a surprisingly active role in immigration cases, he still recognizes that "there is no right to judicial review in many important immigration cases." *Id.* at 522. In particular, "[c]onsidering the lack of independence in the administrative adjudication process, the vesting of complete and unreviewable discretion in the Attorney General regarding whether an alien should be allowed to reside in this country has understandably troubled immigration scholars." *Id.* at 523.

4 *Flores v. Ashcroft,* 350 F.3d. 666 (7th Cir. 2003).

5 Immigration Act of 1990, PUB. L. 101-649, §121, 104 Stat. 4978, 4987-88 (codified as amended at 8 U.S.C. § 1153 (1990)).

holding advanced degrees (or those possessing exceptional ability in the arts, sciences or business) whose work would benefit the national economy, cultural or educational interests of the United States would be *exempted* from the legal requirement that they obtain a job offer from a U.S. employer. Hence, those persons would avoid the long and arduous labor certification process if such application would be in the national interest of the United States.[1]

A major sponsor of this provision was Senator Jesse Helms of North Carolina. In the Senate debate, Helms described the transformation of his State from the time he first took office to the present as "truly remarkable." He reminisced that North Carolina had moved from a dying and stagnant tobacco economy to one led and transformed by the foreign Ph.D.s and M.D.s who had come to live and work in the Research Triangle area of North Carolina and advocated that America needs a policy that encourages skilled workers and people with exceptional abilities to come to our country. Unfortunately, our current system discourages them from immigrating . . . ."[2]

The enactment of the exceptional ability/national interest waiver provision opened a new path for applicants to obtain immigrant visas. In the early 1990s, the INS (USCIS) was deluged with applications in this category, and approvals of petitions were plentiful. This apparently did not sit well with the INS and the Clinton administration. In August of 1998, the Wall Street Journal ran a front-page article mocking the INS for approving anyone with a "pulse" under this category.[3] Citing an "acrobat from Russia who plays a horn while flying through the air, Korean golf-course designers, Russian ballroom dancers and Ghanaian drum makers"[4] as examples of the types of applicants being approved under this category. From there, the INS had enough.

In the same month (August 1998), the INS issued an administrative decision confronting these ambiguities. In *Matter of N.Y. State*

---

1 135 CONG. REC. 758 — 02 (daily ed. July 12, 1989) (statement of Sen. Jesse Helms).
2 *Id.*
3 Barry Newman, *"Alien Notions: The 'National Interest' Causes INS to Wander Down Peculiar Paths — Or How a Roving Acrobat Got a Visa While Doctor Probing Cancer Didn't — Is the Curio Cabinet Closed?," WALL ST. J.*, Aug. 20, 1998, at A1.
4 *Id.*

Department of Transportation ("NYSDOT"),[1] the Board of Immigration Appeals finally transformed the ambiguous concept of 'national interest' into a defined set of conceptual guidelines, delineated below:

1. The alien applicant must be seeking employment in an area of "substantial intrinsic merit;"
2. The proposed benefit must be national in scope; and
3. The alien applicant seeking exemption from the labor certification process must present a national benefit so great as to outweigh the "national interest inherent in the labor certification process."[2]

The impact of the third prong of the NYSDOT prong was the most significant. It allowed the INS to engage in the subjective process of assessing and evaluating any applicant and determining by its own standards which achievements by aliens would "greatly exceed the achievements and significant contributions" of U.S. workers and "exhibit some degree of influence on the field as a whole."[3]

The NYSDOT standard was implemented without any statutory or regulatory changes to the existing exceptional ability provisions, in contravention with the USCIS's own regulation, which explicitly provide requirements for the national interest waiver.[4] USCIS regulations require a showing that to "the alien is an alien of exceptional ability in the sciences, arts or business, the petition must be accompanied by at least *three* of the following" six criteria.

1. An official academic record showing that the alien has a degree, diploma, certificate or similar award from a college, university, school or other institution of learning related to the area of exceptional ability;
2. Evidence in the form of letter(s) from current or former employer(s) showing that he has at least ten years of full-time experience in the occupation for which he or she was sought;
3. A license to practice the profession or certification for a particular profession or occupation;

---

1 22 I. & N. Dec. 215, Interim decision (B.I.A.) 3363 (1998).
2 *Id.*
3 *Id.*
4 *See* Immigrant Visa Petitions, 8 C.F.R. § 204.5(k)(3)(ii) (2007).

4. Evidence that the alien has commanded a salary, or other remuneration for services demonstrates exceptional ability;

5. Evidence of membership in professional associations; or

6. Evidence of recognition for achievements and significant contributions to the field by peers, governmental entities, or professional or business organizations.[1]

Despite these INS criteria, Congress's failure to define "national interest" in its legislation left the door open for the INS to step in and provide a definition. The INS did just that, with the *NYSDOT* decision. Quite remarkably, *NYSDOT* has no basis in the statute Congress passed in 1990, nor is it consistent with that statute. What is worse, the INS's own regulations are in direct conflict with the statutory provision.

Part IV — Failures Inherent to the Current System

Although USCIS presents a particularly compelling case study of the failures inherent in the current system of administrative law, these failures are by no means exclusive to the immigration law context. Practitioners in many areas of administrative law routinely run up against a system that elevates executive power above congressional intent and the fair adjudication of administrative hearings.[2]

Across the board, congressional oversight has been a failure, as the record would certainly seem to indicate, particularly when looking at agency rules and regulations. Congress has shown little interest and demonstrated little effectiveness in curbing agency abuse and disregard for legislative enactments. It is indeed difficult to place faith in an institution with such a disappointing record and

---

1 *Id.*

2 *See, e.g.*, Jason D. Vendel, Note, *General Bias and Administrative Law Judges: Is There a Remedy for Social Security Disability Claimants?*, 90 CORNELL L. REV. 769, 770-75 (2005) (finding bias in social security claims administrative hearings); Clean Water Action et al., *Continuing Dereliction of Duty: How Michigan's Environmental Agency Defies the Law and the Public* 7 (Feb. 8, 2001), *available at* http://www.mec-protects.org/deqreport2.pdf (finding bias in environmental hearings before administrative law judges); *cf. also* Cynthia M. Ohlenforst et al., *Annual Survey of Texas Law: Taxation*, 59 SMU L. REV. 1565, 1570 (2006) (stating that one recent survey found that in general "[t]axpayers had few successes before administrative law judges").

whose members rarely read the text of legislation prior to voting on whether to enact a particular bill.

Presidential administration and the growth of executive power have reached unprecedented levels in the last decade. One author has described it as "the shift from congressional preeminence . . . to presidential preeminence."[1]

Whether it is the use or abuse (depending on one's viewpoint) of executive orders or direct White House control over specific agencies through the EOP, executive power is on the rise. With all due respect to Professor Kagan's argument that more power must, by necessity, be placed in the executive branch, it is difficult to see the benefits of more executive control when recent executive branch policies have included incarceration without due process, agency rulemaking without effective review, and stripping courts of powers of judicial review.[2] All of these policies have been made possible by the seemingly limitless power of the unitary presidency.[3]

Since most agencies already have some form of internal administrative review, either by administrative judges or agency officials, an increase in internal review is not likely a viable solution. The problem with internal administrative review is that it is often a mere technicality because the decision-maker does not have the true independence and impartiality that is needed to reach fair resolutions.[4] Some commentators have stated that this lack of in-

---

1 Joseph Cooper, *From Congressional to Presidential Preeminence: Power and Politics in Late Nineteenth-Century America and Today, in CONGRESS RECONSIDERED* (Dodd & Oppenheimer, eds.,2005)

2 Donald S. Dobkin, *Court Stripping: Limitations on Judicial Review of Immigration Cases*, 28 JUST. SYS. J. 104 (2007).

3 Indeed, the current administration has shown a willingness to find ways to expand executive power even in those rare instances where Congress attempts to exercise oversight. *See* CHARLES TIEFER, *supra* note 24, at 238 ("Among more exotic tactics, the administration has *sabotaged congressional overseers* by accusing them of unpatriotically violating intelligence rules . . . .") (emphasis added).

4 *See, e.g.,* Vendel, Note, *supra* note 88, at 770 ("[F]ew will deny that bias inevitably seeps into their decisionmaking process. . . . With some ALJs, however, bias more than seeps. It gushes."). *But see* Harold J. Krent & Lindsay DuVall, "*Accommodating ALJ Decision Making Independence with Institutional Interests of the Administrative Judiciary*," 25 J. NAT'L ASS'N ADMIN. L. JUDGES 1, 26-27 (2005) (citing Administrative Procedure Act (APA), 5 U.S.C. §§554(d), 557(d)(1) (2000)) ("[T]he APA largely protects ALJs at the federal level from external influence. Agencies that employ ALJs cannot hire or fire them, except for cause. Nor do the agencies set their pay. In addition, ex parte discussions are limited in order to

dependence and impartiality allows administrative law judges to engage in "lawless decision-making."[1] For instance, a large coalition of environmental groups in Michigan has noted that "EPA staff have confirmed they identified . . . administrative law judge rulings that are inconsistent with state and federal law."[2]

For the most part, administrative judges have not demonstrated sufficient independence from the agency over which they review. Because they remain employees of the executive branch and can be removed at any time for virtually any reason, the visible lack of any semblance of judicial independence substantially undercuts their credibility. Indeed, according to ethicist Professor James Moliterno, our current system requires administrative judges to "recognize that their role demands adherence to agency policy and goals."[3] In other words, administrative judges cannot even be independent because they are, in fact, *legally* bound to adhere to agency policies:

Clearly, administrative judges must follow the agency's legislative rules, but, perhaps more controversially with some administrative judges, they must also follow other statements or indicators of agency policy. They are, after all, agents of the agency and have no independent authority to divine policy. The only true source of their authority is the agency itself, and their judgment must be informed by the agency's and not their own sense of good policy. This aspect is an important distinction between administrative judges and Article III judges and their state court counterparts.[4]

---

prevent even the appearance of impropriety. Although Congress can reduce pay for ALJs as a group or eliminate their jobs altogether, Congress cannot readily pressure any individual ALJ to reach a particular decision.").

1 Vendel, *supra* note 88, at 770.

2 *Clean Water Action, supra* note 88, at 7, *available at* http://www.mecprotects. org/deqreport2.pdf.

3 James Moliterno, *The Administrative Judiciary's Independence Myth*, 41 WAKE FOREST L. REV. 1191, 1192 (2006); *see also* Patricia E. Salkin, *Judging Ethics for Administrative Law Judges: Adoption of a Uniform Code of Conduct for the Administrative Judiciary*, 11 WIDENER J. PUB. L. 7, 22 (citations omitted) ("Whether it is appropriate to apply the same code of judicial conduct to constitutional court judges, ALJs, and hearing officers is a matter of considerable debate. One argument advanced against the application of the code of judicial conduct considers that, since *ALJs may be viewed as nothing more than employees* whose job it is to help the agency

4 Moliterno, *supra* note 95, at 1199.

Further, "as a matter of practice, Presidents commonly tell agencies what they want them to do,"[1] and those priorities are likely to carry weight with administrative judges. Although administrative judges are also bound by legal requirements that they act "in an impartial manner" when presiding over hearings,[2] it is difficult to see how employees can truly be impartial to decisions made by their employers.

Generally, administrative law judges lack proper insulation and independence from administrative agencies. This is especially true for Immigration Judges, who lack even the theoretical "statutory independence" that Congress has granted to other administrative law judges.[3] An example is the recent removal of more than a dozen Immigration Judges by the executive branch for an alleged failure to deport aliens at a fast enough pace.[4] Indeed, a recent analysis revealed that "[t]he Bush administration [has] increasingly emphasized partisan political ties over expertise . . .

In selecting the judges who decide the fate of hundreds of thousands of immigrants," despite laws that preclude such considerations.[5] Professor Brian Slocum has noted that since 2002, the Attorney General has taken numerous actions "that reinforced the no-

1 Sargentich, *supra* note 16 at 7.

2 Administrative Procedure Act, 5 U.S.C. § 556(b) (2000).

3 Jeffrey S. Lubbers, *Closing Remarks, Holes in the Fence: Immigration Reform and Border Security in the United States*, 59 ADMIN. L. REV. 621, 627 (2007). But see Nina Bernstein, *Immigration Judges Facing Performance Reviews*, New York Times, Aug. 10, 2006, *available at* http://www.nytimes.com/2006/08/10/washington/10immig.html (quoting an immigration law judge who claims that judges like herself "by statute are supposed to be neutral, independent decision makers").

4 *See, e.g.*, Carol Marin, *Patronage "Crime" Does Pay – for Justice Dept.*, CHI. SUN-TIMES, Mar. 25, 2007, at B6, *available at* http://findarticles.com/p/articles/mi_qn4155/is_20070325/ai_n18757004 ("Just as we like to think our U.S. attorneys function with a high degree of independence despite being political appointees, we like to think that our judges do, too. But immigration judges work for the Justice Department, not the federal courts. Their boss is also Alberto Gonzales. And just as Gonzales and the Bush administration are being accused of pursuing a blatantly political agenda with regard to the fired U.S. attorneys, they have been accused of doing the same thing with regard to immigration judges, who basically do what the administration wants them to do."); *see also* Bernstein, *supra* note 98 (noting that a new policy of requiring "performance evaluations raised serious concerns for the independence of judges")

5 Amy Goldstein & Dan Eggan, *"Immigration Judges Often Picked Based on GOP Ties,"* WASH. POST, June 11, 2007, at A1.

tion that Immigration Judges and BIA members are *employees* of the Department of Justice *rather than independent adjudicators*."[1] To make matters worse, "[a]ll the judges appointed during this period who arrived with experience in immigration law were prosecutors or held other immigration enforcement jobs."[2] Hiring practices such as these make it difficult to believe that immigration judges are truly neutral and independent.

Because agencies sometimes base hiring — and firing — practices on the outcomes they expect to receive from administrative judges, these judges are under enormous pressure to keep their employers happy. In general, the administrative judges themselves have never been comfortable being in this position, and they have for many years "sought to ensure their independence in resolving cases brought under myriad administrative schemes at both the federal and state levels."[3]

This lack of independence becomes all the more problematic because the employers of administrative judges are the very agencies that are most likely to appear as parties (usually defendants) before the judge: "Often, one of the litigants before the administrative judge is the judge's employer."[4] The administrative judge is then asked to pass judgment on the very same agency that has the power to terminate the judge's employment.

It is no wonder that when litigants brings lawsuits against agencies, the litigants often take it as a given that they will lose before the administrative judge.[5] These litigants thus focus much of their attention on the first appeal to a federal district court. This process might be acceptable if they were guaranteed to get a fair hearing at

1 Brian G. Slocum, *Courts vs. the Political Branches: Immigration "Reform" and the Battle for the Future of Immigration Law*, 5 GEORGETOWN J.L. & PUB. POL. 509, 515 (2007) (emphasis added).

2 Goldstein & Eggan, *supra* note 101.

3 Harold J. Krent & Lindsay DuVall, *"Accommodating ALJ Decision Making Independence with Institutional Interests of the Administrative Judiciary,"* 25 J. NAT'L ASS'N ADMIN. L. JUDGES1, 1 (2005).

4 Moliterno, *supra* note 95, at 1195.

5 *See, e.g.,* Andrew W. Barnes, Comment, *"Building on Michigan Wetlands After* In re Ocedek: *Analyzing On-site and Off-site Alternatives Under the 'Feasible and Prudent Alternative" Test of Part 303 of the NREPA,* 2006 MICH. ST. L. REV. 511, 514 n.12 (noting that environmental groups blame some of their losses at the administrative level on administrative law judges being "pro-development").

the district court level. The problem is that losing at the administrative level can poison later proceedings. For instance, on appeal, later courts will defer to an administrative judge's findings of fact "unless they are unsupported by substantial evidence on the record."[1] Cases are often won or lost based on how the initial decision-maker views the facts, which are often open to various interpretations. All of this makes it crucial that the initial judicial decision-maker be truly independent and impartial. Administrative judges under the current system cannot fulfill this role.

If administrative judges are not fit to hear these cases, should we instead go straight to the federal district courts? The problem here is that the current federal court system is already too overburdened to hear the large volume of administrative agency matters.[2] And federal judges, in many instances, have shown a lack of interest in hearing such cases.[3]

Part V — Prescriptions For Lawfulness

This then leaves the creation of new Article III courts with the power of judicial review as the only sensible solution to the current state of affairs, if only by default. We need to create a new corps of federal judges who only hear cases involving agency rules and regulations. Congress could easily create such a corps.[4] Indeed, in 1983, the Judicial Administration Division of the American Bar Association passed a resolution "favoring the passage of legislation to

---

1 *E.g., O'Leary v. Brown-Pacific-Maxon, Inc.,* 340 U.S. 504, 508 (1951).

2 *See, e.g., Carden v. Arkoma Assoc.,* 494 US 185, 207 (O'Connor, J., dissenting) ("[O]ur federal courts are already seriously overburdened."); Jeff Jones, *"Court Overload,"* ALBUQUERQUE J., Nov. 5, 2005, at A1 ("Illegal immigrants are . . . pushing the entire New Mexico federal court system near a breaking point. The sheer volume of immigration cases filed in federal courts is crushing."). *But see* Robert L. Ostertag, *"New York and the Law,"* 10 EXPERIENCE 6, 7 (2000) ("[I]n 1998, . . . New York's statewide judicial system absorbed more than 3.4 million new cases. During that same time the entire federal district court system throughout America took in fewer than 300,000 just the year before, a more than 11-to-1 ratio. One wonders sometimes why federal judges feel overburdened.").

3 Donald S. Dobkin, *"The Diminishing Prospects for Legal Immigration: Clinton through Bush,"* 19 *St. Thomas L. Rev.* 329 (2006).

4 Article III of the Constitution expressly permits Congress to create lower federal courts. U.S. Const. art. III, § 1 ("Congress may from time to time ordain and establish [lower federal courts.]").

establish federal administrative law judges *as an independent corps.*"[1] More recently, Congress has considered legislation to bring independence to Immigration Judges.[2] Thus, it is not unreasonable to suggest that Congress should go further and actually take the steps necessary to create a new corps of federal judges.

Creating a new corps of federal judges to hear administrative matters is the only way to reinstate proper checks and balances and to ensure what scholars deem to be a central constitutional principle — namely, that "no particular actor should be dominant."[3] When a unitary executive branch has the power to influence all levels of agency decisions, including those made by administrative judges, the executive branch has become dominant in a way that violates basic principles of the separation of powers. A new corps of federal judges would help reinstate constitutional principles regarding the separation of powers. Professor Robin Arzt has argued forcefully for the need to create an independent body to adjudicate social security claims:

> When an agency . . . exclusively uses rulemaking proceedings to set policy, rather than also using adjudications to set policy, there no longer is any rationale for keeping the adjudicatory function within the agency. The Congressional interest in providing a check on . . . enforcement powers . . . is best served by having benefits entitlement determinations decided by an independent adjudicatory agency.[4]

The same rationale supports moving other agency decisions away from administrative judges and toward a new corps of independent federal judges.

In addition to establishing necessary checks and balances, the creation of a new corps of federal judges would have at least three additional major (and related) practical advantages over the cur-

---

1 Moliterno, *supra* note 95, at 1228 (2006) (citing Victor W. Palmer, "*The Administrative Procedure Act: After 40 Years, Still Searching for Independence,*" *JUDGES' J.* 34, 39 (Winter 1987)).

2 *See* Comprehensive Immigration Reform Act of 2006, S. 2611, 109th Cong. § 229 (2006).

3 Sargentich, *supra* note 16, at 6.

4 Robin J. Arzt, "*Recommendations for a New Independent Adjudication Agency to Make the Final Administrative Adjudications of Social Security Act Benefits Claims,*" 23 J. NAT'L ASS'N ADMIN. L. JUDGES 267, 271 (2003).

rent system. First, the new corps of federal judges would have the requisite independence needed to insulate their decisions from political influence. Second, these judges would also have an opportunity to develop expertise in adjudicating administrative matters. Third, as a result of greater independence and expertise, this new corps of judges would be more likely to decide cases correctly at the outset and thereby help relieve the federal docket by decreasing the amount of work that must be done on appeal.

Judicial independence is foundational to any effort to adjudicate matters fairly and without bias. The drafters of the U.S. Constitution required that all federal judges be insulated from political pressures by life tenure and salary protection.[1] Similarly, the first Canon of the Code of Conduct for United States Judges, entitled *A Judge Should Uphold the Integrity and Independence of the Judiciary*, requires the following of all federal judges:

An independent and honorable judiciary is indispensable to justice in our society. A judge should participate in establishing, maintaining, and enforcing high standards of conduct, and should personally observe those standards, so that the integrity *and independence* of the judiciary may be preserved. The provisions of this Code should be construed and applied to further that objective.[2]

The importance of judicial independence is in fact so ingrained in the minds of most Americans that most of us simply take it for granted that an independent judiciary is crucial to the fair resolution of disputes. We should not deprive litigants in administrative disputes from the benefits of an independent judiciary.

Critics of this approach could argue that a new corps of federal judges would not actually create a truly independent judiciary. After all, the new federal judges would presumably be appointed by the President and would therefore be likely to share many of the political viewpoints of the executive branch. Nevertheless, the ap-

---

1 U.S. CONST. art. III, § 1 ("The Judges, both of the supreme and inferior Courts, shall hold their Offices during good Behaviour, and shall, at stated Times, receive for their Services, a Compensation, which shall not be diminished during their Continuance in Office.").

2 *CODE OF CONDUCT FOR UNITED STATES JUDGES* Canon 1 (2000) (emphasis added).

pointment process for Article III judges is far less likely to produce a partisan judiciary than the current process for appointing administrative judges. After all, Article III judges must be confirmed by the Senate, which theoretically acts as a check to prevent the President from appointing partisan candidates, especially when the Senate is controlled by a different political party. Also, we know from experience that the constitutional protections afforded to Article III judges — life tenure and salary protection — really do allow judges to act independently without fear of political recourse. For instance, U.S. Supreme Court Justice David Souter was appointed by a politically conservative president (George H.W. Bush), and Justice Souter is now considered to be one of the most liberal judges on the bench.

A new corps of federal judges to hear administrative matters would also allow these judges to become experts in adjudicating administrative matters. The benefit of expertise is related to judicial independence. Although some would argue that administrative judges are already experts in adjudicating the matters that come before them, a more realistic (if somewhat cynical) view is that a lack of judicial independence prevents administrative judges from developing this expertise. Rather than searching for the correct legal answer, an administrative judge might be more concerned with finding ways to interpret the law in a way that justifies whatever actions were taken by the agency that employs the judge.

Creating a new corps of federal judges would also help relieve the current burden on federal courts. Although an overburdened federal judiciary is not an excuse for failing to ensure the proper administration of justice,[1] it is all the better if we can find a way to ensure fair adjudication of administrative matters without overburdening the federal court system. The creation of a new corps of federal judges to hear administrative matters does precisely that. In fact, because the new corps of federal judges would be truly independent and impartial, these judges would be more likely to reach

---

1 *See, e.g.,* Danné L. Johnson, *SEC Settlement: Agency Self-Interest of Public Interest*, 12 FORD. J. CORP. & FIN. L. 627, 678 n.233 (2007) (noting that in general even when federal courts are overburdened, "public interest in adjudication should not give way to an overburdened system").

the proper outcome at the outset. This would be a major improvement, given that immigration judges, for instance, are currently reversed more than twice as often as other civil trial court judges.[1] The improper initial adjudication of these cases "has placed a greater burden on federal courts."[2] If immigration cases and other administrative cases were tried initially by truly independent judges, we could expect to see far fewer appeals — and less work to do on those appeals — than under the current system of agency-employed administrative judges. As a result, this new corps of federal judges goes a long way toward helping relieve the federal docket.

1 *See* Slocum, *supra* note 102, at 518, n.48 (citing Judge Posner in *Benslimane v. Gonzales,* 430 F.3d 828, 829 (7th Cir. 2005), as "comparing the reversal rate in immigration cases of 40% to the 18% reversal rate in other civil cases").
2 *Id.* at 525.

5. Enforcement: Arguments and Misconceptions

In June 2010, Eric Balderas was a student at Harvard studying molecular and cellular biology in hopes of a career in cancer research. Within days, he became a controversial figure after attempting to use his Mexican consulate card and Harvard I.D. instead of his passport, which he said he had lost, in boarding a plane to Boston from his hometown of San Antonio Texas. Upon discovering his undocumented status, U.S. immigration officials took him into custody, and he faced possible deportation to the country he had left when was 4 years old. The case garnered international attention, and two weeks later, the U.S. Immigration and Customs Enforcement (I.C.E.) said that they would not pursue his deportation.

"I aspire to find a cure for cancer... I hope to succeed someday because this will be a way for me to contribute," Balderas told *America's Voice*.[1]

Not everyone was happy that he remained here. *FamilySecurityMatters.org* contributing editor Paul Hollrah had this to say about Balderas:

---

1 Hastings, Maribel, "DREAM Act: How many like Eric Balderas Until the Senate Acts?," *America's Voice*, (June 17, 2010), http://act.americasvoiceonline.org/expressionengine.php?/blog/entry/dream_act_how_many_like_eric_balderas_until_the_senate_acts

"One wonders, if such people are so interested in 'making a difference' in the world, why do they insist on bringing that passion to the United States where we're all pretty comfortable and where we're not looking for foreigners to make a lot of 'difference' in our lives? Why don't they stay at home and try to make a 'difference' in the hell-holes where they were born? Maybe they come because they heard some idiot say, 'My friends, we live in the greatest nation in the history of the world. I hope you'll join me as I try to change it.' After hearing that bit of insanity they just couldn't resist coming to see what it was all about."[1]

The enforcement of immigration laws is a polarizing topic, and the closer one looks, the more confusing are the facts. We have already seen in recent years an increase in the number of people deported, more workplace raids, a stepping up of enforcement. Yet, in July of 2010, the Obama administration sued Arizona over the state's strict immigration law.[2] The Arizona legislature passed the controversial law to try to cut back the illegal immigrants who cross its border from Mexico and to cut down on crimes such as drug trafficking. The administration, however, argued that the new law (S.B. 1070) was unconstitutional and would deplete law enforcement resources. In a 5–4 decision, the Supreme Court ruled that sections 3, 5(C), and 6 of S. B. 1070 are preempted by federal law, striking down sections that required legal immigrants to carry registration documents; allowed state police to arrest any individual on mere suspicion of being an illegal immigrant; and made it a crime for an illegal immigrant to hold or seek a job in the state. The Court unanimously upheld provisions allowing Arizona state police to briefly detain to investigate the immigration status of an individual stopped or arrested if there is reasonable suspicion that individual is in the country illegally. Cases challenging racial profiling are meanwhile allowed to proceed through the courts.

"As a direct result of failed and inconsistent federal enforcement, Arizona is under attack from violent Mexican drug and im-

---

1 Hollrah, Paul, *"The Eric Balderas Caper,"* Family Security.org, (June 10, 2010), http://www.familysecuritymatters.org/publications/detail/the-eric-balderas-caper
2 *Arizona v. United States*, 567 U.S. __ (2012), Opinion (6/12/2012) available at, http://www.supremecourt.gov/opinions/11pdf/11-182b5e1.pdf

migrant smuggling cartels," said Gov. Jan Brewer, a Republican, in a prepared statement. "Now, Arizona is under attack in federal court from President Obama and his Department of Justice."[1]

This is the crux of the immigration enforcement policy; we have none. Instead, we have a number of arguments as to why we should increase enforcement. We have an administration that argues against stepping it up, but does so just the same.

It's Not True That We Aren't Enforcing the Immigration Laws. We Are.

The U.S. Immigration and Customs Enforcement (ICE) deported 392,000 people in the 2011 fiscal year.[2] That total is up markedly from the Bush administration's 358,886 total for 2008 and 202,842 for 2004. In 1990, the number was 30,039.

The number of those deported between Oct. 1, 2009, and June 30 of 2010 is nearly twice as much as it was in the same period ending June 30, 2005, according to research by the Transactional Records Access Clearinghouse at Syracuse University.[3] The increase in worksite arrests in 2008 was twelve times those of 2002. According to *The Washington Post*, the government's immigration enforcement programs hold more detainees each night than the Clarion Hotel chain, operates nearly as many vehicles as Greyhound has buses, and flies more people out of the country each day than do many small U.S. airlines.[4]

Furthermore, according to ICE data, the Obama administration is devoting more of its resources to removing those who have committed serious crimes. In Fiscal Year 2011, the agency removed 188,000 known "criminal aliens," a record high.[5] During the first

---

1 CBS, "*Jan Brewer: We will beat all law suits against Arizona illegal immigration law*," (July 7, 2010), http://www.cbsnews.com/8301-503544_162-20009831-503544.html .

2 Simansky, John and Sapp, Leslie, US Department of Homeland Security Office of Immigration Statistics, *Immigration Enforcement Actions, 2011* http://www.dhs.gov/sites/default/files/publications/immigration-statistics/enforcement_ar_2011.pdf.

3 Syracuse University, Transactional Records, http://trac.syr.edu/immigration/ .

4 Hsu, S. and Sylvia, M. "Border Policy's Success Strains Resources." *Washington Post.* (February 2, 2007), http://www.washingtonpost.com/wp-dyn/content/article/2007/02/01/AR2007020102238_pf.html.

5 Simansky & Sapp, *Ibid.*

nine months of the 2010 fiscal year, 136,714 criminal aliens' were deported. In 2008, the number was 85,334. The figure for the first nine months of the 2010 fiscal year for removals of non-criminal aliens was 142,321, compared to 169,429 at the same time in 2008.

Although the term "criminal alien" conjures images of gun-toting foreigners intent on destruction, in some states being convicted of drunk driving three times is a felony. So is attempting to enter the United States illegally after being deported. Yet all of these "crimes" are incorporated in the statistics that constitute the "criminal alien" population. These stats are misused because they paint a picture of the illegal alien population as being higher in criminality than the general American population at large. However, if one strips out the immigration crime of trying to enter the U.S. illegally after being deported, one finds that the illegal immigrant population has a significantly *lower* crime rate that the general population in the U.S.

Immigration and Customs Enforcement (ICE)

- ICE was established in 2003 as part of the federal government's response to the Sept. 11 attacks. The Homeland Security Act mandated breakup and replacement of the legacy Immigration and Naturalization Service (INS).
- ICE is one of three DHS bureaus created to replace INS. The other two are U.S. Customs and Border Protection (CBP) and Citizenship and Immigration Services (USCIS).
- ICE is the second largest federal law-enforcement agency in the U.S. after the FBI.
- ICE is in charge of investigation, arrest, detention and deportation at the border and throughout the interior of the U.S.
- ICE comprises Homeland Security Investigations (HSI), Enforcement and Removal Operations (ERO), and Management and Administration (MA)
- ICE has approximately 19,000 employees in more than 400 offices worldwide
- ICE has an annual budget of more than $5 billion in 2010
- The 2005 ICE annual budget was $3,557,454.

According to a February 2010 report by the U.S. Department of Homeland Security, the U.S. illegal immigrant population declined by almost 1 million.[1] The number of illegal immigrants living in the United States dropped to 10.8 million in 2009 from 11.6 million in 2008. This was the second consecutive year of decline and the sharpest decrease in at least three decades.

Yet criticism of the President and Homeland Security chief Ja-net Napolitano increased greatly since Arizona's 2010 law (SB 1070) gave police more power to detain immigrants. Gov. Brewer criti-cized Obama for assigning only 1,200 National Guard soldiers to the entire Mexican border, with 524 in Arizona. Senator John McCain said it was the failure of the Obama administration to "secure our borders" that forced Arizona to enact SB 1070 in the first place.[2]

In justifying the legislation, Brewer said the administration had "simply turned a blind eye to the issues that Arizona is being over-run by illegal immigration, terrorizing the citizens."[3]

Yet, the numbers don't agree.

What is the policy of the United States? How can we ramp up enforcement, yet on the other hand, file a lawsuit to block the im-plementation of the Arizona law? Surely it must be more than just a turf war. Makes one wonder: who's running the insane asylum? The problem may be more of a consequence of the Congress allocating more and more money to DHS and ICE for enforcement. Congress is and has been absolutely obsessed with pandering to voters who overwhelmingly favor greater enforcement. No wonder enforce-ment has dramatically enforced. They are so many more DHS and ICE agents than just five years ago, they seem to be tripping all over each other!

---

1 Michael Hoefer, et. al., US Department of Homeland Security, Office of Immigration Statistics, "Estimates of the unauthorized immigrant population residing in the United States," January 2010, http://www.dhs.gov/xlibrary/assets/statistics/publica-tions/ois_ill_pe_2010.pdf

2 KVOA.com, "McCain on SB 1070," (May 26, 2010), http://www.kvoa.com/news/senator-mccain-on-sb1070/

3 USA Today, "Arizona Governor Blames Obama for Failing on Immigration Reform," (April 23, 2010), http://content.usatoday.com/communities/ondeadline/post/2010/04/obama-arizonas-immigration-law-could-undermine-basic-notions-of-fair-ness/1#.UKA4ZWd5iEc

The Criminality Argument

In 1994, California's Proposition 187 was passed with 59 percent of the statewide vote in 1994. It declared that "the people of California ... have suffered and are suffering economic hardship ... personal injury and damage caused by the criminal conduct of illegal aliens in this state."[1]

Although the proposition was later overturned by a federal court as unconstitutional, it expressed a commonly shared belief about immigrants and crime.

"Illegal immigration puts pressure on public schools and hospitals, it strains state and local budgets, and brings crime to our communities," said George W. Bush in his address to the nation in May of 2006.[2] Contrary to these assumptions, the illegal immigrant population has less criminality than the general public at large.

A 2008 report by the Public Policy Institute of California found that immigrants are far less likely than U.S.-born Californians to commit crime. Although people born abroad made up approximately 35 percent of California's adult population, they accounted for only about 17 percent of the adult prison population, the report showed. Among men ages 18 to 40 — the demographic most likely to be imprisoned — those born in the U.S. were 10 times more likely than foreign-born men to be incarcerated.[3]

The Security Argument

Many in favor of strong enforcement believe those immigrants are a security risk and that stepping up those policies will deter terrorists. However, there are as many with green cards inside as outside the U.S. In 2009, 36,231,554 non-immigrants were admitted at U.S. borders. Of those, 32,544,098 were temporary visitors

---

1 California Proposition 187 - Limits the Privileges and Rights of Legal Aliens, (Adopted Nov. 1994), http://www.wwnorton.com/college/history/archive/resources/documents/ch37_03.htm

2 *Bush's Speech on Immigration, The New York Times*, (May 15, 2006), http://www.nytimes.com/2006/05/15/washington/15text-bush.html?pagewanted=print

3 Butcher, Kristin and Piehl, Anne, *"Crime, Corrections, and California: What Does Immigration Have to Do with It?,"* Public Policy Institute, February 2008, http://www.ppic.org/main/publication.asp?i=776

---

for business or pleasure.[1] Does anyone really think that adequate background checks had been done on these 36 million visitors? The only way we could effectively increase security in the alien population would be to close the border, and we would be in a depression within twenty-four hours.

The Drain Argument

Of the approximately 3 million students who graduate from U.S. high schools each year, approximately 65,000 are illegal immigrants. In March 2009, the Development, Relief and Education for Alien Minors Act was introduced in the United States Senate and House of Representatives. Pioneered by Sen. Orin Hatch and Sen. Richard Durbin, the DREAM Act would allow qualifying undocumented young people who graduate from U.S. high schools to be eligible for a six-year long conditional path to citizenship. Students would obtain a temporary residency for six years. During this time, each student would have to earn a college degree or complete at least two years toward a bachelor's degree or two years of military service.

"Hopefully, the people who support me will call their Senators and Representatives in order to achieve something because the DREAM Act is what would save us all," Eric Balderas said. "Whatever happens during my hearing, good or bad, is only a temporary solution because I would not get permanent residency."[2]

Some opponents of the DREAM Act say Balderas was a willing tool to create awareness and support. They say the act will reward illegal immigrants who will take from the U.S. without contributing back to our economy. As do many who support tough enforcement, they see immigrants as a financial burden demanding free medical care and free educations. Yet a U.S. Government Accountability Office study found that approximately 75 percent of undocumented immigrants work for employers who withhold income taxes, Social

---

1 Monger, Randall, *et al.*, U.S. Department of Homeland Security, Office of Immigration Statistics, *Nonimmigrant Admissions to the United States, 2009*, http://www.dhs.gov/xlibrary/assets/statistics/publications/ni_fr_2009.pdf
2 Hastings, M., *Ibid.*

Security and Medicare payments. According to the Social Security budget, they contribute between $7 billion and $8 billion annually.[1]

In order to get those jobs, many use false Social Security numbers. They pay into the Social Security system for benefits they will never collect. They pay taxes although they will never file a return or receive a refund. Even immigrants who are compensated in cash still pay phone, gas, alcohol, auto, and sales tax and if they rent, property tax.[2]

Not *Do* We Enforce, But *How* We Enforce

Jason "J.T." Ready embodies the anger regarding Arizona's illegal immigration. The former marine and his fellow militia members have donned body armor and gas masks and showed up in the Arizona desert in July of 2010. Ready declared that they were declaring war on "narco-terrorists" as well as looking for illegal immigrants.

Ready says he identifies with the National Socialist Movement, a group that, according to the Associated Press, believes only non-Jewish, white heterosexuals should be American citizens, and that everyone who isn't white should leave the country "peacefully or by force."

One would acknowledge the government's right to seal its own borders. You can't condone illegality; you can't have laws you don't enforce. But here's where the situation gets sticky. Do we have the right to seal our borders? Yes. Enforce our laws? Of course. But do we want big fences and troops? Do we really want ICE SWAT teams going into every Denny's in the country handcuffing cooks and busboys with a gun at their necks while we're eating our scrambled eggs? Any discussion of enforcement must involve the kind of image we want to portray.

---

1 Porter, Eduardo *"Illegal Immigrants Are Bolstering Social Security With Billions"*. New York Times, April 5, 2005, http://www.nytimes.com/2005/04/05/business/05immigration.html?ex=1270353600&en=78c87ac4641dc383&ei=5090

2 Congressional Budget Office (CBO), *The Impact of Unauthorized Immigrants on State and Local Governments*, December 6, 2007, http://www.cbo.gov/publication/41645

The U.S. Needs Workers

Illegal immigration exists because for many, it is the only way. Only seasonal workers qualify for the temporary worker programs, and only five thousand permanent residence visas for low-skilled and other workers are issued per year. To obtain any kind of working visa is extremely difficult, if not downright impossible. Because opportunities for legal immigration are limited, the worker demand is high if only because fewer low-skilled native workers are available in this country. Between 1996 and 2008, the number of U.S. workers without a high school education dropped by 2.3 million, and the number of U.S. workers with only a high school education fell by 1.3 million, or 4 percent.[1]

In her unsuccessful bid to win the Republican nomination for governor of California, Meg Whitman listed measures she would employ to target illegal immigrants. "Modeled after drug seizure raids, Meg will institute a system where state and local law enforcement agencies conduct inspections of workplaces suspected of employing undocumented workers."[2] Offenders would have to pay a fine and have their business licenses suspended for 10 days. By the third offense, their licenses would be permanently suspended, and the fine would be "substantial."

Except that, by law, workplace inspections are a federal responsibility. Whitman soon learned that state raids were not popular with the California Farm Bureau, which had endorsed her early in the primary election. In July of 2010, she softened her approach. According to her revised policy, she would wait until after Congress approved a law requiring all employers to screen workers with an electronic ID verification.

Whitman is just another example showing that, when it comes to policy, apparently no one no one is clear or consistent. And that that includes the government.

---

1 Sherk, James, "*Technology Explains Drop in Manufacturing Jobs*," Heritage Foundation, ftn 7, (October 12, 2010), http://www.heritage.org/research/reports/2010/10/technology-explains-drop-in-manufacturing-jobs

2 Ferriss, Susan; "*Meg Whitman backs away from immigration inspection plan*," McClatchey Newspapers, (July 16, 2010), http://www.mcclatchydc.com/2010/07/16/v-print/97639/meg-whitman-backs-away-from-immigration.html

In the next chapter, we're going to examine one of the major reasons for our economic decline: our viewing of potential citizens as liabilities instead of as potential customers from whom we can benefit.

6. The Edict of Non-Reviewability

Imagine this: after several years of enduring the protracted, expensive and arduous legal immigration process from your country of origin, you arrive at the United States Embassy for an interview. For reasons beyond understanding, a consular officer whom you've never met before and who has had no prior relationship to your case casually informs you that your visa will not be issued. Case closed. There's the door. Thank you very little.

Baffled, you try to contact the embassy by email, phone or registered mail to obtain the grounds for denial. You track backward over every step and review every item needed for the visa. Everything is in order. That can't be it. You try to contact anyone related to the case. No one responds. Shockingly, when you try to take action to obtain any information on the grounds of your denial, you find there is no path for legal recourse. You are not a citizen and have no rights under U.S. laws.

The judicial system has virtually no inclination to intervene in, or even review, the process, continually refusing to view these cases unless a U.S. attorney or other U.S. persons directly related to you take action in your stead.

You are cast adrift, having followed every procedure, adhered to all rules and standards, and submitted every document and detail. Despite years of labor, investment and dedication, you, as they say, are [blank] out of luck.

In the nuttiest of nutshells, immigration applicants to the United States — the land of the free — can be denied visas on any grounds, or no apparent grounds at all, and have no option for legal recourse and no guarantee that they might receive a reason for their denial.

No Process is Due Process

In 1950, at the height of the Cold War, and before the sweeping Civil Rights and Women's Liberation Movements, the Supreme Court decided in the case of *Knauff v. Shaughnessy* that "whatever the procedure authorized by Congress is, it is due process as an alien denied entry is concerned."[1] The effect of this simple and vague ruling echoes throughout agency hallways across the world. Given that Congress has never specified how "due process" applies to aliens or visa applicants, the concept does not, in fact, exist. In practical application, the power of an immigration consular officer trumps the human rights of immigrants to challenge their denials for citizenship in a court of law. Since immigrant applicants at U.S. Consulates abroad are by definition not U.S. citizens, and outside the U.S., federal courts are not applicable and no courts outside the U.S. would bear jurisdiction. It's a neat Catch-22 as long as you're not caught on the receiving end.

In the heightened fears of the post 9/11 world, we operate very much as we did in the Cold War, sanctioning absolute governmental power over the rights of visa applicants, despite all the advancements in human rights made since that time. The case of *Knauff v. Shaughnessy* codifies the doctrine of "consular non-reviewability" or, perhaps more aptly, "consular absolutism" — the exercise of unconditional agency authority over decision-making process. While

---

1 *Knauff v. Shaughnessy*, 338 U.S. 537 (1950), http://www.jstor.org.emils.lib.colum.edu/stable/.

this inviolable practice was quick in its application, it was long in the making.

More than sixty years after the court decision, there is still virtually no consistent legal recourse for immigrants arbitrarily rejected in the process of obtaining visas abroad, and almost uniformly the courts extend more consideration towards the consular entity than the visa applicants or other plaintiffs themselves.

Under the doctrine of consular non-reviewability, "a U.S. citizen raising a constitutional challenge to the denial of a visa is entitled to a limited judiciary inquiry regarding a reason for the decision. As long as a reason given is facially legitimate and bona fide, the decision will not be disturbed."[1]

One might suspect that a "facially legitimate and bona fide" reason is an almost impossibly vague standard that allows for a wide range interpretation, to say the least, granting the consular office unlimited power over the judicial system, which again allots "limited judicial review" for immigrants in the first place. If ever a court wanted to write itself out of legal proceedings, this is the model to follow.

Despite the argument that consular non-reviewability is a necessary power for Congress in the wake of the 9/11 attacks, its roots date back even further than the Cold War, demonstrating with each passing year its lack of relevance as well as its origins in racist attitudes.[2] The Treaty of 1880 and the Chinese Exclusion Act of 1882 marked the first restrictions on immigration, the latter suspending naturalization of Chinese citizens for 10 years.[3] It was in these openly discriminatory documents that the Supreme Court ceded to other branches of government the sweeping opportunity to govern immigration. Congress was ceded "plenary power" over immigration, with the State Department actions toward visa seekers deemed to be all but "non-reviewable" as the unfettered exercise of foreign policy. Essentially, legal recourse was being institutionally denied on the basis of race and reactionary politics, with an

1 http://integrity-legal.com/legal-blog/us-visa-immigration-the-doctrine-of-consular-absolutism-or-consular-nonreviewability/

2 Churgin, Michael, "Mass Exoduses: The Response of the United States," at 311

3 Ibid., "Mass Exoduses."

extremely restrictive view by the courts of their own jurisdiction and powers in such matters. The courts have in effect abdicated to the other branches the power to determine how much process is due, and with it breadth of constitutional protection. Because these politics were rooted in a restrictive view of constitutional protection weighed down by racist ideologies, it became practice to deny any legal recourse towards potential immigrants abroad despite manifest injustice of outcomes and no compelling public interest to support arbitrary exclusionary measures.

As the decades progressed, subsequent court cases would decide other grounds on which immigrants could be denied citizenship, usually rooted in attitudes that blatantly excluded the underprivileged or political undesirables, literally institutionalizing a system of inequality and lack of cognizable rights for foreigners.[1]

The More Things Change...

Nearly a century and a half later, these policies have affirmed the foundation of denying immigrants the right to have their cases heard in United States courts, only allowing for limited judiciary review. While it is not necessarily surprising that this practice stems from outdated, racist perceptions, these origins should provide all the more reason to redefine our judiciary processes.

Simply put, in direct contradiction to the principles of rights of all persons on which this country was founded, the doctrine of consular non-reviewability allows for discriminatory practices to take place in our courts, stifling not only human rights for immigrants, but damaging our international relations as well. It's high time that we reexamine a patently unfair doctrine that serves no one adequately or well.

A Brief History Lesson

In order to understand the historical context that allowed for consular non-reviewability to emerge from our court systems, in addition to understanding how such a doctrine has both hindered due process for immigrants as well as violated basic human rights of

---

1 Wucker, Michele, *Lockout* (Public Affairs: New York, 2006) at 30.

citizens, one must analyze several key court decisions and legislative actions in conversation with this argument.

Firstly, one turns to the precepts of the Chinese Exclusion Act, which was the beginning of a long line of acts that entrenched this legislatively and judicially created doctrine of non-reviewability and legislative limits on judicial review, "court-stripping" measures, as a mainstay in immigration law. The Act, passed in 1882, coincided with widespread efforts in Congress and the States to restrict immigration along with the franchise of Blacks and other minorities through "Jim Crow" Laws; in the case of Asians, the effort to exclude Asians from citizenship and franchise was particularly complete.

That same year, Congress passed an Act to create a head tax and placed further restrictions on immigrants:

> All idiots, imbeciles, ... insane persons ... persons likely to become a public charge; persons afflicted with tuberculosis or with a loathsome and contagious disease; persons not comprehended within any of the foregoing excluded classes who are found to be and are certified by the examining surgeon as being mentally or physically defective ... persons who admit their belief in ... polygamy, anarchists, or persons who believe in or advocate the overthrow of the government by violence force.[1]

It was these restrictions, along with exclusions based on race, which granted consular officers the ability to deny visas for practically any reason based on a wide interpretation and broad powers of discretion afforded. Even though immigrants and citizens alike began to challenge visa denials that were granted on unfair or unspecified grounds, the judicial system would continue to largely wave its own powers and interest in the subject matter. In general, obtaining preliminary jurisdiction of review became as or more difficult than proving the merits of any particular claim, in any suit for consular review.

In *United States ex rel. London v. Phelps*, it was noted *in dicta* that it was "beyond the jurisdiction of the court" to review the refusal of a visa.[2] In *Ulrich v. Kellogg*, it was declared that no immigration law

---

1 Wucker, *Ibid.*

2 *Ibid.* at 290. Scholars have noted that the *Phelps* decision is rather ambiguous on this point, since "the court does not clearly state whether it lacked personal

provides for an official review at the hands of the court. In *Knauff v. Shaughnessy*, it was decided that it was "not within province of any court ... to review the determination of the political branch of the government to exclude a given alien."[1]

Essentially, the court system signed off their ability to check the consular offices as a branch of government in favor of ever-more inculcated exclusionary, white-washing politics.

As if these decisions weren't sufficient to provide absolute rule over arbitrary immigration practices, consider the more recent case of *Kleindienst v. Mandel*, which cited the *Chinese Exclusion Case* as still-valid foundation for the doctrine of consular absolutism or non-reviewability; indeed, it was also the first court decision to officially recognize the doctrine and give it that name.

In the case of *Mandel*, not only was a racist and outdated legislative act itself *cited as the general doctrinal foundation for its decision*, but in particular the decision upheld the denial of a temporary visa based on purported Communist affiliations, a common reason for denial that would be a clear violation of any U.S. citizen's right to freedom of speech. This tissue of reasoning also providing means for denial of U.S. visas to prominent writers and intellectuals such as Gabriel Garcia Marquez, Pablo Neruda, Jorge Luis Borges, among others.[2]

The Court decision of *Kleindienst v. Mandel* was explicitly and knowingly based in exclusionary politics and violations of human rights, and according to any other standard of U.S. law should not be the grounds for any legitimate court decision. This stark contrast, alone, provides reason enough for complete overhaul and re-evaluation of the doctrine.

jurisdiction or subject matter jurisdiction over the parties." Timothy R. Hager, Comment, *Recognizing the Judicial and Arbitral Rights of Aliens to Review Consular Refusals of "E" Visas*, 66 TUL. L. REV. 203, 213 (1991) (citing Stephen Legomsky, IMMIGRATION AND THE JUDICIARY: LAW AND POLITICS IN BRITAIN AND AMERICA 145 (1987)).

1 *United States ex rel. Knauff v. Shaughnessy*, 338 U.S. 537, 543 (1950).

2 Shaprio, Steven "*Ideological Exclusions: Closing the Border to Political Dissidents*" http://www.jstor.org/pss/1341100.

When In Doubt, Obfuscate

So what the heck is "a facially legitimate and bona fide reason," anyway? As stated in *Kleindienst v. Mandel*, the reason court review was unavailable was because the government had put forth "a facially legitimate and bona fide reason" for its actions.[1] This effectively permits limited court review and intervention and usually only to affirm government denial.

Mandel wouldn't have even had his day in court if the case hadn't been brought before court by American colleagues who claimed the decision violated their own First and Fifth Amendment rights to association with the excluded party. This is problematic because it does not address legislation regarding broader immigration policy, and serves only to fight interpretation of vague policy with interpretation of our constitutional rights, without being necessarily applicable as precedent to the fundamental human rights of the immigrant.

Since Mandel's case, there have been several similar instances which have upheld the doctrine of non-reviewability. The rare exception is found in *Allende v. Shultz*, a 1983 case in which a U.S. visitor's visa had been denied to Hortensia Allende, the widow of the late Chilean President, who was found by the U.S. Consul in Mexico to be "prejudicial to the United States" for her supposed Soviet Communist affiliations. Her case was taken to court by a group of U.S. lawyers, religious, and human rights organizations, and she prevailed under the *Mandel* test after it was shown that there were no facially legitimate or bona fide reasons to hold that Allende was actually a security threat to the United States. Her radical affiliations and inclinations were shown to be merely speculative, the result of Cold War-era reaction rather than any hard evidence of subversive intent. This was the first instance in which the court overturned a consular officer's decision, the first evidence challenging the notion of consular absolutism.

Although *Allende* showed a way for challenging consular decisions in court, the lack of definition of qualifications for "a facially

---

1 *Kleindienst v. Mandel*, 408 U.S. 753, 765 (1972).

legitimate and bona fide reason" in the *Mandel* case still leaves the consular office with a vast and elastic reservoir of unchecked power. The doctrine itself is filled with sufficient loopholes that allow resistance to various constitutional and procedural challenges, the latter of which is more typical of court review because it usually involves purely legal questions of statutory interpretation, a simpler route to dismissal of a claim than determining whether someone's constitutional rights have been violated.

In the case of *Martinez v. Bell*, it was decided that the courts have the power to decide the constitutionality of a given provision in a visa determination without violating consular non-reviewability under the Immigration and Nationality Act. The trial court found that while it lacked jurisdiction over the outcome of the particular decision to deny an immigrant visa, it nonetheless has "jurisdiction to direct the Department of State to do that which it is both authorized and required to do," which was to duly consider the application. Subsequently, constitutional rights to process have been separated from consular absolutism in the eyes of the court.[1]

On the other hand, consular officers are to be subject to a wide array of procedural requirements under statues and regulations, to the point that they should not be allowed to deny or grant visas purely of their own discretion — as previous legislation had been interpreted to allow.

The Pocket Veto

The most basic function of consular officers is that they are required to either deny or issue a visa. It is hoped that they would make these decisions based on sound policy and transparent regulation. However, even the first function of the officer — issuing or denying a visa — is often simply set aside, failing even to issue a written decision at all.[2]

In *Patel v. Reno*, the United States Consulate in India simply refused to act on visa applications for the children of a naturalized citizen. In this instance, as in *Martinez*, the court denied the govern-

---

1 See, e.g., *Martinez v. Bell*, 468 F. Supp. 719, 725–26 (D.C.N.Y. 1979).
2 406 F. Supp. at 165.

ment's request to apply the doctrine of non-reviewability due to the consul's refusal to afford a determination in clear violation of procedure. The court maintained that jurisdiction could exist "when the suit challenges the authority of the consul to take or fail to take action as opposed to a decision taken with the consul's discretion."[1] This effectively means that the consular officer does not have the discretion to avoid procedure that must be followed by an officer, but if a procedure exists, the discretionary determination (insofar as discretion is actually employed) of the consul remains essentially non-reviewable.

While some courts have implied that they do not intend to follow the decision of the case of *Patel v. Reno*, demonstrating a knowingly inconsistent application of the doctrine of consular absolutism, hopes for current applicants are slimmer than ever.

What Next

At this point, the need for legislative overhaul of this doctrine should be self-evident. The doctrine of Consular Non-Reviewability is deeply problematic, flawed, and filled with more holes than a ton of Swiss cheese. Its applications are often contradictory, hypocritical, and vague. It is time to finally undo the damage caused by this outdated, fundamentally discriminatory doctrine and, instead, lay out a course of legal action for immigrants who wish to have their visa cases reviewed.

It is time for the United States to accept the rule of law applies to official U.S. Government determinations made outside the territory of the United States and that power of visa determination is not purely the unfettered exercise of foreign policy, but is instead subject to Due Process of law as is the rest of the federal government's administrative determinations.

---

1 *Patel v. Reno*, 134 F.3d 931–32 (9th Cir. 1998)

7. The Economic Impact of Closed Borders

Imagine a political debate in a hotly contested election. The moderator asks the candidates "What is your plan to bring the U.S. out of the current economic recession?" It would not be surprising to hear someone respond, "My plan is simple: close the borders. We shouldn't be handing out government services to immigrants or letting them take jobs away from Americans. The more jobs Americans have, the better the economy."

That response would likely garner cheers from members of the audience, given the widespread public opposition to immigration that prevails throughout the U.S. and many other industrialized countries.[1] It certainly makes for a compelling sound bite. It seems like simple math — more immigrants means more people competing for a limited number of jobs, which would presumably decrease each person's chances of getting a job.

The only problem with this analysis is that it is dead wrong. Closing the borders would not help our economy — it would destroy it. Despite widespread opinion among the American public that undocumented immigrants take advantage of government

---

1 Cornelius, Wayne A. & Rosenblum, Marc R., "Immigration and Politics" (2004), Center for Comparative Immigration Studies, UC San Diego, at 99, http://es-cholarship.org/uc/item/24t4f706.

services and generally harm the U.S. economy, scholars have made clear that such a belief is "undeniably false."[1] For some reason, immigration policy in the U.S. "tends to be governed more by economic fallacies than by facts."[2]

Indeed, those who have studied this issue have concluded that what actually harms our economy is anti-immigration policies, and that the economy would benefit greatly from a more open-border policy. Historically, immigration has always been a key component of the success of the U.S. economy, and that remains true today. In fact, although the current economic recession can be attributed to many things, it has clearly been exacerbated by the crackdown on immigration that followed the September 11 attacks.[3] It follows that lessening restrictions on immigration would help lift us out of the current economic recession.

How important is immigration to the U.S. economy? The numbers are quite staggering. By some accounts, undocumented immigrants alone currently contribute around $800 billion to the U.S. economy every year in goods and services consumed combined with what they produce for their employers.[4] Even using the most conservative estimates, immigration contributes at least $10 billion annually to the U.S. economy, and that is under the current system and its many existing restrictions on immigration.[5]

In one of the most fascinating studies to date, a group of economists recently analyzed the economic effects of closing our borders entirely for one year. Prompted by speculation that a bird-flu epidemic could lead the U.S. to take drastic measures, such as closing our borders for a significant period of time, these economists

---

1 Lipman, Francine J., *"Taxing Undocumented Immigrants: Separate, Unequal, and Without Representation,"* Tax Lawyer, vol. 59, pp. 813-866 (2006) at 815-816.

2 Obhof, Larry J., *"The Irrationality of Enforcement? An Economic Analysis of U.S. Immigration Law,"* Kansas Journal of Law and Public Policy, vol. 12-Fall, 163-190 (2002) at 163.

3 Shatniy, Natalya, "Economic Effects of Immigration: Avoiding Past Mistakes and Preparing for the Future," The Scholar: St. Mary's Law Review on Minority Issues, vol. 14, 869-911 (2012) at 872.

4 O'Connell, Patricia, *"A Massive Economic Development Boom,"* BusinessWeek (July 18, 2005), http://www.businessweek.com/magazine/content/05_29/b3943005_mz001.htm.

5 Cornelius, *Ibid.* at 103.

wanted to know what would happen to our economy in those circumstances.

The results were shocking. According to the study, the total loss of closing our borders for one year would be $2.359 trillion.[1] Granted, that number includes the economic impacts of a host of activities beyond legal and illegal immigration. In particular, in addition to evaluating the impacts of a one-year shutdown of immigration, the study evaluated the effects of a one-year shutdown of all international air travel in and out of the U.S., all international commodity trade (except gas and oil delivered via pipeline), and all cross-border shopping. But the model also used very conservative estimates, including assuming that domestic production will increase greatly to accommodate losses in the international sector, and the study did not take into account the enormous costs related to the actual implementation of border closures (assuming such a thing is even possible). Focusing solely on the economic effects of closing our borders to legal and illegal immigration, the study concluded that halting legal immigration for one year would cost the U.S. economy over $10 billion, and halting illegal immigration would lead to an additional loss of over $2 billion.[2] This includes over 3 million lost jobs across a wide variety of sectors.[3]

Also, these studies are limited in that they look only at the continuation of our current, overly restrictive immigration policies. When we look at what is possible under less restrictive policies, we get a better view of the true effects of our current immigration policies. For instance, a study by the CATO Institute concluded that legalizing the more than eight million undocumented workers in the U.S. would eventually lead to roughly $180 billion in annual benefits.[4] Stricter border controls, by contrast, would lead to permanent economic losses of around $80 billion per year.[5]

---

1 Gordon, Peter; Moore, James E. II; Park, Ji Young; and Richardson, Harry W., "The Economic Impacts of International Border Closure: A State-By-State Analysis" (2009) at 2, http://research.create.usc.edu/nonpublished_reports/30 .

2 Gordon *et al., Ibid.* at 6-7.

3 *Ibid.* at 18-19.

4 Dixon, Peter B. & Rimmer, Maureen T., "*Restriction or Legalization? Measuring the Economic Benefits of Immigration Reform*" (CATO Institute Aug. 13, 2009) at 13.

5 Dixon & Rimmer, *Ibid.* at 9.

And those are just the tangible impacts that can be monetized. There are many other impacts of closed borders that would harm the U.S. economy in ways that should not be underestimated, even if we cannot put a dollar value on it. For instance, a closed-border policy is often reciprocal. When the U.S. imposes restrictions on immigration, other countries are more likely to restrict the travel of American citizens to other countries. And restrictions on travel are much more than an inconvenience — such restrictions have a devastating effect on the U.S. economy.

One reason that travel restrictions are so damaging to the U.S. economy is that it hampers service industries that need regular access to their international customers. Currently 70 percent of Americans work in service industries.[1] And that number is likely only going to grow, given present trends away from an industrial-based economy and toward a service-oriented economy. In 2011, the U.S. exported $612 billion in services.[2] Although that number is quite high, it is much lower than it could be. The reason is that the U.S.'s strict immigration and travel controls, along with its protectionist trading policies, are often reciprocated by other countries. According to some, if borders were more open everywhere, the result would be a net gain in jobs for the U.S., as well as a more than doubling of exported services that would add as much as $800 billion to the U.S.'s GDP.[3]

So to recount, just one of the effects of our current closed-border policies is to deprive our economy of as much as $800 billion in lost service exports, and if we moved to even more of a closed-border policy by shutting down immigration and deporting undocumented workers, it could cost our economy an additional $800 billion.

Given the devastating effects that closed-border policies have on the U.S. economy, and the enormous economic benefits that immigrants bring to the U.S., shouldn't we look to increase immigration as one way out of the current economic recession? The answer

---

1 Paparelli, Angelo A., *"Immigration Protectionism Costs America Billions"* (Apr. 14, 2012), http://www.nationofimmigrators.com/immigration-protectionism/immigration-protectionism-cost-america-billions/ .
2 *Ibid.*
3 *Ibid.*

is undoubtedly a resounding "Yes." Unfortunately, the reality is that economic recessions often have precisely the *opposite* effect and lead to a crackdown on immigration.[1]

Why does our immigration policy lead us to do precisely what is most harmful to our economy? If we were truly as concerned with economic growth as our politicians purport to be, then why are we constantly restricting immigration and thereby depriving ourselves of the vast economic benefits that flow from increased immigration?

Part of what is going on here is that the vast majority of the American public has deep-rooted assumptions that color how it views immigration and immigrants. These substantial misconceptions often come from an emotional response to a perceived threat.[2]

To understand how misconceptions and underlying assumptions color the American public's view of immigration, consider the riddle about a father and his son that are in a car accident. Both are badly hurt. They are taken to separate hospitals. When the boy is taken in for an operation, the doctor says "I cannot do the surgery because this is my son." The riddle asks, How this is possible?

Although some people come up with the answer right away, this riddle gives most Americans pause, if not stumping them altogether. The answer to the riddle is simply that the doctor is the boy's mother. What makes this a riddle at all, let alone one that many people have difficulty solving, is that it exploits the powerful and deep-rooted assumption that most doctors are men. That assumption colors our view of the riddle and blinds many of us to what is otherwise an obvious answer.

So how does this relate to immigration policy and closed borders? The vast majority of Americans have an underlying deep-seated assumption that immigrants are always employ*ees* (and unskilled ones at that), never employ*ers*. Or to use Ayn Rand's terminology — which has been making a resurgence in recent years — we tend to view immigrants as job seekers, rather than job creators. And, worse yet, we too often assume that immigrants are unskilled laborers, even though many of them are highly skilled professionals,

---

1 Shatniy, *Ibid.* at 877.
2 Cornelius, *Ibid.* at 103.

managers, and, perhaps most importantly, entrepreneurs. Further, even when just looking at those immigrants who are lower-skilled laborers, the net impact that they have on the U.S. economy is overwhelmingly positive.

When we can put our assumptions aside and look at the pure economics of immigration, a clear picture emerges. Immigrants are a primary driver and a crucial component of the U.S. economy. Our universities and our corporations want to — and need to — recruit and retain people from all over the world, not just those who happen to have been born in the U.S., and closed-border immigration policies are crippling the ability of U.S. industries to compete in a global marketplace.

Let's take a more detailed look at the true economic impact of closed borders — a term used here to refer to any immigration policy that places restrictions on the free flow of foreign-born nationals who seek to enter the U.S. To fully examine the economic impact of closed-border policies, it is helpful to consider what happens to the U.S. economy when our immigration policies prevent the following four groups of people from entering or remaining in the U.S.: (1) undocumented immigrants; (2) international students; (3) highly skilled immigrant workers; and (4) immigrant entrepreneurs. In each instance, closing our borders to one of these groups has a direct and significant negative impact on the U.S. economy. And closing our borders to all four groups has a combined impact that all but assures a bleak future for the U.S. economy.

The Economic Impact of Shutting Out and Deporting Undocumented Immigrants

Let's begin with the argument that the American public is likely to be most skeptical of — the idea that closing our borders and shutting out undocumented immigrants would harm the U.S. economy. Even assuming that undocumented immigrants are for the most part lower-skilled workers, the research has made clear that they have been, and continue to be, a boon to the U.S. economy, not a drain on it. And, even more interestingly, undocumented immigrants have a net positive influence on the employment of native-born workers.

The idea that immigrants take jobs away from others rests upon the false notion that there is a fixed number of jobs in the American economy. This zero-sum argument ignores the reality that the economy is constantly in flux, and that immigration generally increases job opportunities for native-born citizens.

There are a number of ways in which undocumented immigrants are a positive force for the U.S. economy. To begin, undocumented immigrants increase the U.S. population, which in turn increases demand for local consumption of goods and services. This helps all U.S.-based businesses and thereby boosts economic growth across all sectors.

Second, undocumented workers help increase the labor force in the U.S., where the baby boomers are beginning to retire, which will in turn cause worker shortfalls in a number of sectors. The current economic recession — and, in particular, the stock-market collapse that began in 2007 and drained many baby boomers' retirement accounts — has led many ageing Americans to continue working longer than they had planned. The result is a temporary respite from this expected worker shortfall, but the shortfall has merely been delayed, not avoided. A number of economists have expressed concern that the U.S. economy is suffering from an inadequate labor force. Recent projections from the U.S. Bureau of Labor Statistics have noted that the growth rate of the U.S. labor force is only around half the rate we experienced just 20 years ago.[1] Immigration helps address the shrinking labor force.

By expanding the labor force, undocumented workers also lower the prices of consumer goods.[2] Many of the jobs that immigrants take are jobs that are not available to others or that native-born workers are unwilling to do. Indeed, some sectors of our economy, such as agricultural production, depend on the existence of an undocumented population of immigrants. And it is undisputed that American consumers are able to purchase fruits, vegetables, grains,

---

1 Paparelli. *Ibid.*
2 Cornelius, *Ibid* at 103.

and other food products for cheaper prices as a direct result of efficiencies that the agriculture sector gains from hiring undocumented immigrants.[1]

Another way that undocumented immigrants contribute to the U.S. economy is that they often make payments into Social Security, Medicare, and unemployment insurance funds, even though they are unlikely to ever benefit from those programs.[2] And those contributions are not trivial. According to some estimates, undocumented workers add roughly $7 billion every year in Social Security payments that they will never collect.[3]

In addition, all undocumented workers pay the same sales taxes as everyone else, and around 75% of them pay income taxes as well.[4] Of the undocumented immigrants who pay income tax, less than a third of them seek tax refunds.[5] And those who do seek refunds find that they are ineligible for certain tax benefits such as the refundable portion of the Earned Income Tax Credit. The result is that for taxes, as with Social Security, undocumented immigrants often put much more into the system than they will ever get out.

As for the oft-made assumption that undocumented workers take jobs away from low-skilled native-born workers, the evidence simply does not support that notion. A recent study in fact noted that undocumented workers help expand the U.S. economy, allowing low-skilled native-born workers to move up the occupational ladder.[6] If it sounds too good to be true that an influx in unskilled immigrant workers would lead unskilled native-born workers to obtain higher-level jobs, history tells us this has already happened. During the "Great Migration" of the early 1900s, an influx of immigrants spurred a dramatic increase in the number of native-born workers who stayed in high school through graduation and took other measures to increase their work skills.[7]

---

1 Obhof, *Ibid.* at 166.
2 Cornelius, *Ibid.* at 103.
3 Weber, *Ibid.* at 779.
4 Obhof, *Ibid.* at 175.
5 *Ibid.*
6 Lipman, *Ibid.* at 817.
7 Dixon & Rimmer, *Ibid.* at 11.

Also, although lower-skilled immigrants may find little room for economic mobility, particularly if they are undocumented, their children will have a chance at receiving the education and skills necessary to be a much larger driving force in the economy that is handed down to the next generation. It is well-known that first-generation immigrant parents with limited educational backgrounds are often the fiercest advocates for making sure that their children get the education that they never had. While far too many of the children of native-born U.S. citizens take education for granted or even resent having to go to school, the children of immigrants generally recognize what a an incredible opportunity it is to have the chance to receive an education. This attitude makes a significant segment of this population much more likely to work hard at school and take the steps necessary to further their education in any way possible. As a result, the dividing line between lower-skilled immigrants and higher-skilled immigrants is not always so clear, since "low-skill immigrants frequently turn into high-skill immigrants as first-generation American parents invest in their children's education."[1] The result is an even greater positive impact on the U.S. economy.

Finally, by contrast to the enormous economic benefits the U.S. receives from undocumented immigrants, the process of closing our borders is incredibly expensive. For instance, Congress recently took actions to allocate $600 million just for one year of border security.[2] It is also well documented that increased border controls have a more tragic — and uncountable — cost that comes in the form of an increase in migration-related deaths.[3]

Given that undocumented workers provide crucial benefits to the U.S. economy, it is not surprising that a number of scholars have questioned why the federal governing is "spending billions of dollars" on border-closing and deportation efforts that, if successful, would "cause the worst economic disaster in the history of the

---

1 Florida, Richard, *The Flight of the Creative Class: The New Global Competition for Talent* (2005) at 84.

2 Giovagnoli, Mary, "The Immigration Balancing Act: ICE Memo and High Removal Statistics Reveal a Stacked Immigration System," *Immigration Impact* (Aug. 27, 2010).

3 Cornelius, *Ibid.* at 111.

United States."[1] In short, just as the U.S.'s banks are too big to fail, closed-border and other anti-immigration policies are too big to succeed.

The Economic Impact of Shutting Out International Students

Another way that U.S. immigration policy is negatively impacting our economy is through restrictions on student visas. Richard Florida describes undergraduate and graduate students as "canaries in the talent mine," and notes that "the countries that succeed in attracting them gain advantages on multiple fronts."[2] This student population is highly mobile, and the best and brightest in the world have a number of options for where to take their intellectual prowess. As a result, when restrictive immigration policies delay and deny student visas, students can — and do — look elsewhere.

American responses to September 11 led to a sharp decrease in the number of visas available to foreign-born students seeking to attend college or graduate school in the U.S. In 2002, the number of student visas issued fell by 20% (the largest drop ever recorded), and in 2003 the U.S. decreased that number by an additional 8% (the second largest drop ever recorded).[3] This sent a clear message to foreign students that even if they were accepted to an American university, they could not count on actually being able to attend college or graduate school there.

That was the explicit message that the U.S. government sent by denying and delaying the issuance of student visas. But it sent another message as well — it told the best and brightest young minds from around the world that the U.S. was not welcoming of them. It told them that the U.S. saw them first and foremost not as the future engineers, scientists, doctors, computer programmers, or entrepreneurs, but as potential terrorists. This added another dimension to the delays and denials of student visas. Not only was the Department of Homeland Security placing explicit roadblocks

---

1 Shatniy, *Ibid.* at 911.
2 Florida, *Ibid.* at 147.
3 *Ibid.* at 12.

in the way of students who sought to bring their talents to the U.S., but it was also putting up more subtle barriers to entry.

Imagine the psychological impact on someone who is smart enough to get into one of the U.S.'s top universities, only to be told that she must first prove beyond a doubt that she is not a terrorist. If the U.S. makes it this difficult to get permission just to enter the country to study, what would it be like try to stay there permanently once school was complete? Would they forever be unwelcome or treated as second-class citizens? Would the U.S. government let them travel home for vacations, or would they have to stay at all times within U.S. borders for fear of running into trouble when trying to re-enter the country? Suddenly the idea of attending school in the U.S., let alone moving there permanently once school was complete, no longer seems like the best option.

As word got out that the U.S. was being more scrutinizing in its issuance of student visas, student advisors at some of the world's best secondary schools saw the writing on the wall and started encouraging their best students to apply to Oxford, Cambridge, and McGill, rather than Harvard, Yale, and MIT. Thus, unsurprisingly, for the fall of 2004 admission cycle, 90% of U.S. graduate schools reported a sharp drop in the number of applications from international students — on average, they were receiving nearly one-third fewer international applications.[1] The number of international students applying to take the Graduate Record Exam (GRE) in 2004 also decreased by one-third.[2]

During this same time period, the top British, Australian, and Canadian universities were courting these same international students. As a result, the universities in these countries were receiving "their best applicant pools ever, made up increasingly of students who say they are applying there instead of the United States."[3] In short, the increased restrictions on student visas in the U.S. had the direct effect of sending global talent to other countries. The best students in the world were "starting to vote with their feet, pursu-

---

1 *Ibid.* at 12.
2 Florida, Ibid. at 12.
3 Ibid. at 13.

ing alternative options in other countries."[1] And in the meanwhile, a number of other countries were doing everything they could to continue — and even accelerate — this trend and make sure that as many of the most talented students came to study at their universities rather than in the U.S.[2]

The fact is that the U.S. is no longer the only game in town when it comes to the best universities, job opportunities, and overall quality of life. The U.S. "position as the global magnet for the world's most talented and hardest working is in jeopardy."[3] This is a dramatic change from the last few decades, during which the U.S. has had a steady stream of immigrants who would be willing to do just about anything to be able to live here and take a shot at the "American dream." Most people in the U.S. assume that immigrants will always want to come to our country, and that the role of immigration policy is to place restrictions on what would otherwise be an overwhelming flow of immigrants. But increasingly restrictive immigration policies and greater enforcement of those policies — whether through unexplained and unreviewable visa denials or through heightened efforts toward deportations — has made the prospect of coming to the U.S. much less appealing. While many would still make the effort to come to the U.S., legally or illegally, during an economic boom, the potential upside to living here is hampered by the current economic recession. Tellingly, a recent report showed that even the "four-decade tidal wave of Mexican immigration" to the U.S. is over, and that today more Mexicans are *leaving* the U.S. than entering it.[4]

When the U.S. is no longer at the top when it comes to where immigrants want to study, work, and live, our economy suffers greatly. Consider the timing of the current recession, which most economists say began in 2007. While the housing, mortgage, and

1 Ibid. at 109.

2 Partnership for a New American Economy & Partnership for New York City, "Not Coming to America: Why the U.S. Is Falling Behind in the Global Race for Talent" (2012), http://www.renewoureconomy.org/sites/all/themes/pnae/not-coming-to-america.pdf at 14-16.

3 Partnership for a New American Economy, *Ibid.* at 1.

4 Bahrampour, Tara, "For first time since Depression, more Mexicans leave U.S. than enter," The Washington Post (April 23, 2012).

banking crises are undoubtedly the primary culprits when it comes to pointing fingers at the causes of our current recession, there is no doubt that other factors have contributed to its severity.

One factor in particular that appears to have been overlooked is the cumulative effect of increasingly restrictive immigration policies in the years following September 11. Take student visas, for instance. As noted earlier, beginning in 2003, the U.S. denied and delayed student visas, leading to a sharp decline in the number of foreign-born students in our universities. This almost certainly contributed to the recession that began just four years later.

Although Russian-born Sergey Brin came to the U.S. when he was younger, it was during his time in graduate school that he met Larry Page and the two of them decided to start a company called Google. Many other successful high-tech companies have been founded by undergraduate and graduate students. This is not surprising. No matter how demanding studies may be, there is little doubt that, compared to being in the work force, the student life provides greater time and freedom to explore new ideas and try out new projects.

Had we let more international students into our undergraduate and graduate schools during this last decade, how many new high-tech startup companies would they have founded? If we had not closed our borders to so many talented students, would we have become a global leader in industries that other countries currently control? Did we miss out on the world's next Google or on other opportunities that would have lessened the impact and duration of the current recession? We will never know.

But while we cannot know with certainty how big the impact was, it is safe to say that our economy was harmed greatly when the U.S. government chose to increase restrictions on student visas. As one scholar has noted, "when we talk about losing brain- and people-power, we should remember that it doesn't have to be many brains or people to have a serious effect; the loss of just a few leading inventors, entrepreneurs, or venture capitalists can hurt a great deal."[1]

---

1 Florida, *Ibid.* at 111.

The Economic Impact of Shutting Out Highly Skilled Immigrant Workers

In addition to deterring the best and brightest students from attending undergraduate and graduate school here, U.S. immigration policies place inexplicable restrictions on the granting of visas and green cards to highly skilled immigrant workers that our corporations want to hire. Over 20% of immigrants are managers and professionals.[1] Their contributions to the U.S. economy are disproportionately high, and the economy would benefit much more if we allowed additional highly skilled immigrants to enter the country.

The U.S. is desperately in need of employees that are trained in certain highly specialized fields, such as science, technology, engineering, and mathematics (often collectively referred to as "STEM"). The STEM fields have produced new jobs at a much higher rate than the rate of indigenous talent available to fill these jobs.[2] As a coalition of business groups and universities recently lamented in a brochure aimed at policy makers, "fewer than one if five students are both interested and proficient (17.3%) in STEM subjects."[3] And these figures are unlikely to change anytime soon, given that, of all the academic subjects, the STEM fields are currently experiencing the lowest growth rates among U.S. students.[4] With so few students studying STEM subjects, there is little hope that indigenous talent will be able to bridge the labor shortage in these crucial sectors of the U.S. economy. Indeed, one study projected that by 2018, the U.S. STEM fields will create 2.8 million job openings, around 779,000 of which will require graduate-level training, and that, based on current trends, only around 555,200 native-born workers would be qualified to fill those positions.[5] It is thus expected that U.S. corporations will have to look elsewhere to fill the shortfall of 223,800 qualified employees.

1 Obhof, *Ibid.* at 170.
2 Florida, *Ibid.* at 104.
3 Business Higher Education Forum (BHEF), *"Confronting the STEM Challenge: A New Modeling Tool for U.S. Education Policymakers,"* http://www.bhef.com/solutions/documents/BHEF_STEM_Brochure.pdf. at 3.
4 Partnership for a New American Economy, *Ibid.* at 6.
5 *Ibid.* at 6-7.

The most obvious possibility for bridging that talent gap is by continuing to recruit highly skilled foreign-born students and immigrants. While academics are quick to lament the problem of the "brain drain" keeping developing countries from flourishing, little attention has been given to the enormous benefits the U.S. receives from "brain gain." For instance, U.S. graduate programs in science and engineering have for decades benefitted from a steady stream of the very best international students from the top foreign universities in the world.[1] Whenever someone with any significant education emigrates to the U.S., that person's country of origin has effectively subsidized economic growth in the U.S.[2] It is therefore nothing short of baffling to think that every day we choose to turn down those free subsidies by enforcing over-restrictive immigration policies.

Scholar and attorney Peter Landis recently surveyed immigration studies from the Harvard Business School, the National Foundation for American Policy, the Peterson Institute of International Economics, and the National Science Board, and concluded that "it is evident that our increasingly restrictive immigration policies seriously jeopardize our economy and put the U.S. at a significant competitive disadvantage.[3] His article notes that immigrant inventors have contributed to more than 25% of U.S. global patent applications, and that the evidence makes clear that restrictive immigration policies hamper technological innovation.[4] His article also explains several of the many reasons that immigrants have been, are, and will continue to be crucial to the success of the U.S. economy.

Highly skilled immigrants are crucial to allowing our corporations to compete in a global marketplace. And it is difficult to underestimate the extent to which the U.S. economy depends on our corporations being able to compete in a global marketplace. When a U.S. corporation is unable to compete, its entire operation will

---

1 Florida, *Ibid.* at 101-102.

2 Cornelius, *Ibid.* at 106.

3 Landis, Peter J., Esq., *"Commentary: How U.S. Immigration Policy Hurts the U.S. Economy"* (Aug. 1, 2009), http://landisarn.com/2009/08/01/commentary-how-u-s-immigration-policy-hurts-the-u-s-economy/.

4 Landis, *Ibid.*

close down, leading to massive job losses. Shuttering the doors of a factory has ripple effects throughout the entire economy. Each job loss leads to less consumption by that individual, decreasing overall economic activity throughout the U.S. To make matters worse, the federal budget is hit simultaneously with a double whammy, as each unemployed worker stops paying taxes and starts taking advantage of governmental programs such as unemployment compensation.

In this sense, the biggest threat to the U.S. economy is losing our competitive edge. It is indisputable that a competitive global economy will always reward those corporations that simultaneously (1) retain the most competent work force (2) at the lowest cost. An open-border policy goes an enormous way toward the achievement of both of these goals. A closed-border policy, on the other hand, leads to a less competent work force, since employers are choosing employees from a much smaller pool. It also leads to a work force that requires higher salaries, since a more limited supply of potential employees has the necessary consequence of requiring that corporations pay higher salaries to attract candidates from an artificially limited pool.

When U.S. corporations lose their competitive edge, our place in the global economy is at risk. As Mayor Bloomberg has stated, "We will not remain a global superpower if we continue to close our doors to people who want to come here to work hard, start businesses, and pursue the American dream."[1]

Of course, U.S. corporations are not known for going gently into that good night. If there is a way to keep going, they will find it. When the federal government tells U.S. corporations that they cannot bring the best and least expensive skilled workers to the U.S., our corporations unsurprisingly start looking into outsourcing. If they cannot bring the best workers to their factories and offices, they will send their factories and offices to where the best workers are. For instance, in 2007, when Microsoft was expanding its work force from its headquarters in Redmond, Washington, it chose to open up shop in Vancouver, primarily because it knew that

---

[1] Epstein, Jennifer, *"Bloomberg: U.S. immigration policy is 'national suicide,'"* Politico (June 15, 2011).

the Canadian government would allow Microsoft to hire the most talented software developers in the world.[1] When the U.S. government prevents companies from hiring the employees it wants, "it does not take a rocket scientist to figure out why U.S. jobs are going abroad."[2] Simply put, outsourcing provides U.S. corporations with the competitive advantage that our government denies them.

But outsourcing has devastating effects on the U.S. economy, particularly when compared to keeping jobs at home. As noted, every job that stays in the U.S. leads to increased tax revenue from each employee, as well as consumption from that employee that sends money directly back into the U.S. economy.[3] When immigration restrictions force employers to open factories and offices in other countries to find the qualified labor force they need, the U.S. loses much more than jobs — it also loses all of the tax revenue and consumption that would have gone to the U.S. economy if those employees were working in the U.S.

When the immigration debate is framed in these terms, we see that it is not a choice between giving jobs to immigrants or to native-born citizens. That is a false dichotomy. U.S. corporations are going to find ways to make use of the most qualified labor force at the least expense, regardless of immigration restrictions. The actual choice is between keeping and creating jobs in the U.S. versus sending jobs to other countries. If we want jobs to stay in the U.S., and we want to add more jobs to the U.S. economy, we need a more open-border immigration policy. A closed-border policy necessarily shifts jobs to other countries.

There is a clear connection between the hiring of highly skilled immigrants and the resulting increased job opportunities for native-born workers. The addition of a single highly skilled immigrant to a managerial or other specialized position often allows a company to expand and thereby create many more jobs for others.[4]

1 Landis, *Ibid.*
2 *Ibid.*
3 Shatniy, *Ibid.* at 908-909.
4 National Foundation for American Policy (NFAP), *"Analysis: Data Reveal High Denial Rates for L-1 and H-1B Petitions at U.S. Citizenship and Immigration Services"* (February 2012) at 17, http://www.nfap.com/pdf/NFAP_Policy_Brief.USCIS_and_Denial_Rates_of_L1_and_H%201B_Petitions.February2012.pdf .

For instance, TWMA, a company that handles waste for the natural gas and oil industries, recently stated that it wished to hire 200 to 300 more Americans for its Houston office, but that it could only do so if the government first approved work papers for six foreign engineers that are needed to train the new U.S. staff.[1] Rather than taking away jobs from native-born citizens, the six immigrants that TWMA seeks to hire would create hundreds of jobs for native-born citizens.

Can you imagine the political fallout if the U.S. President or a congressperson suggested denying a company its request to create several hundred new jobs? Yet that is precisely the result of immigration policies that keep TWMA from obtaining the six visas it needs to go forward with its expansion.

It would be one thing if the TWMA example were an isolated incident, but the fact is that similar situations are occurring every day throughout the country. And it is happening even though we know that there is a direct, positive, and statistically significant correlation between job growth and the issuance of H-1B visas for highly skilled immigrants with specialized knowledge. For the largest corporations, a single H-1B visa has been shown to create, on average, around five new jobs.[2] For technology companies with less than 5,000 employees, the effect is even greater.[3]

The U.S. economy is highly dependent upon its role as the global leader of technological innovation and invention.[4] Maintaining that position of leadership is crucial to keeping the U.S. economy going, particularly as the global economy continues to move toward what some have referred to as the Third Industrial Revolution.[5] Few doubt that in the near future, many manufacturing jobs will be able to be done by digital means, such as through the use of 3D printers.

1 Dwoskin, Elizabeth, *"Want to Move a Worker to the U.S.? Good Luck,"* Bloomberg *Businessweek* (June 14, 2012).

2 Weber, David P., *"Halting the Deportation of Businesses: A Pragmatic Paradigm for Dealing with Success,"* Georgetown Immigration Law Journal, vol. 23, 763-813 (2009) at 774.

3 Weber, *Ibid.*

4 *Ibid.* at 773.

5 Mehta, Cyrus, *"Halt America's Decline by Welcoming Skilled and Entrepreneurial Immigrants,"* The Insightful Immigration Blog (May 25, 2012), http://blog.cyrusmehta.com/2012/05/halt-americas-decline-by-welcoming.html

The result will be less demand for manual labor, and increased demand for highly skilled workers, particularly those with expertise in industrial design, engineering, information technology, marketing, and other professional fields.[1]

Richard Florida has described this phenomenon as the "new global competition for talent."[2] He states that the U.S. economy's current competitive advantage over other nations is due in no small part to "a tremendous influx of global talent."[3] Historically, the U.S. economy has been the leader in its openness to new ideas, and this has allowed the U.S. "to dominate the global competition for talent, and in doing so harness the creative energies of its own people — and, indeed, the world's."[4] The global influx of talent was present at the nation's founding, but accelerated greatly in the 1930s, as scientists, academics, entrepreneurs, and others came to the U.S. to avoid the fascism and communism movements in Europe.[5] It has continued since then.

But Richard Florida warns that in this realm, past success is by no means a predictor of the future, and the U.S. will need to work hard to continue to attract the world's best and brightest. Indeed, the U.S.'s edge in technological innovation is already under fire — for instance, one survey has shown that the U.S. operates just six of the world's 25 most competitive high-tech companies.[6] Technology companies and their employees are not the only ones setting up shop in other countries. In response to overly restrictive immigration policies, many scientists, engineers, academics, students, performing artists, professionals, managers, entrepreneurs, and other people who are the drivers of the modern economy are crossing the U.S. off their list when they look at where they want to live and work. Worse yet, some of those who currently live in the U.S. are finding that their industries are better served by leaving the country to go to where the best talent is. According to Richard Florida, "the

---

1 Mehta, *Ibid.*
2 Florida, *Ibid.* at 3.
3 *Ibid.* at 5.
4 *Ibid.* at 4.
5 *Ibid.* at 5.
6 *Ibid.* at 15.

real threat to the American economy is not terrorism; it's that we may make creative and talented people stop wanting to come here."[1]

When the world's best and brightest stop coming to the U.S., it has a number of ripple effects on our economy that are not easily quantifiable. For instance, one aspect of technological innovation and invention that is often overlooked is its connection to diversity in the workplace. Increasing diversity by bringing in people with different backgrounds and experiences has been shown to increase the chances of innovation.[2] Being exposed to new cultures and ideas is crucial to the creative process. Scholars who have studied diversity in the workplace have concluded that seeking different ideas from people of different backgrounds is imperative to economic growth.[3] The historical success of the U.S. economy is often attributed in large part to the "powerful engine" of immigration, which has kept the U.S. "younger, growing, and more innovative than other advanced democracies, and refreshed endlessly by new ideas and global connections."[4]

For all of these reasons, closing our borders to highly skilled immigrants harms innovation and leads to job losses in the United States by encouraging employers to focus job growth on other countries, where they have a more predictable labor supply.[5] And it is not just academics and public-policy groups that have noticed the problem: in March of 2012, a coalition of over 50 companies, including Oracle, Microsoft, and Starwood Hotels, sent a letter to President Obama, warning him that "American job growth and the U.S. economy are being harmed" by restrictive immigration policies.[6]

This call from corporate America was not a new one. When Alan Greenspan testified before Congress in 2009 regarding immigration reform, he spoke forcefully about the importance of increasing the flow of skilled immigrants, and he quoted Bill Gates' earlier message to Congress that "America will find it infinitely more

---

1 Florida, *Ibid.* at 17.
2 Obhof, *Ibid.* at 175.
3 Florida, *Ibid.* at 39.
4 Partnership for a New American Economy, *Ibid.* at 4.
5 NFAP, *Ibid.* at 1.
6 Dwoskin. *Ibid.*

difficult to maintain its technological leadership if it shuts out the very people who are most able to help us compete."[1] Greenspan also echoed Bill Gates' admonition against immigration policies that are "driving away the world's best and brightest precisely when we need them most."[2]

And large corporations like Oracle and Microsoft actually have it easy compared to the frustrations that small businesses face when they try to bring in highly skilled immigrants to help expand their companies. According to a memo that the Department of Homeland Security recently released — only after being required to do so by a court order — immigration officials have targeted small businesses for heightened scrutiny in the visa application process.[3]

"Our immigration policy is national suicide," according to New York Mayor Michael Bloomberg.[4] "We educate the best and the brightest and then we don't give them a green card — we want people to create jobs but we won't let entrepreneurs from around the world come here."[5] Mayor Bloomberg has put together a coalition of high-level officials, including the Mayors of Los Angeles, Phoenix, Philadelphia, and San Antonio, as well as the CEOs of Disney, Marriott, Hewlett-Packard, Boeing, and News Corp., to advocate for overhauling the nation's immigration policy to increase opportunities for immigrants to work in the U.S. and for students from other countries to stay here after they graduate.

It is not surprising that U.S. corporations seek greater access to highly skilled immigrants. Scholars have noted that the U.S. currently suffers from a "sagging indigenous talent base in key science

1 Greenspan, Alan, Statement Regarding Comprehensive Immigration Reform in 2009, *"Can We Do It and How?"* , Senate Judiciary Committee, Subcommittee on Immigration, Border Security and Citizenship, 111th Congress (2009), http://www.judiciary.senate.gov/hearings/testimony.cfm?id=e655f9e2809e5476862f735da147e5ee&wit_id=e655f9e2809e5476862f735da147e5ee-1-2 .

2 Greenspan, *Ibid.*

3 Winograd, Ben, *"DHS Creates Obstacles for Small Businesses Seeking High-Skilled Immigrants,"* Immigration Impact, (June 21, 2012), http://immigrationimpact.com/2012/06/21/dhs-creates-obstacles-for-small-businesses-seeking-high-skilled-immigrants/#more-11223 .

4 Saul, Michael Howard, *"Bloomberg Plans Big Immigration Push,"* The Wall Street Journal (June 23, 2010).

5 Saul, *Ibid.*

and technology fields."[1] Let's talk about the numbers. In the U.S., immigrants account for around 50% of all scientists and engineers with doctorate degrees, and around 67% of the entire scientific and engineering workforce.[2] In other words, for every native-born scientist or engineer working in the U.S., there are two immigrants doing the same work. And there is little chance of that changing anytime soon. In fact, if anything, the U.S. is likely to require an even larger percentage of immigrant workers to fill highly specialized scientific, engineering, and technological positions, because foreign-born nationals are studying those subjects at much higher rates than native-born students. For instance, foreign-born nationals currently account for more than 58% of graduate students studying computer science, and more than 68% of graduate students studying electrical engineering.[3]

These statistics have led columnist Thomas Friedman to question why the U.S. government does not attend graduation ceremonies to hand out green cards to foreign-born students obtaining diplomas from top technological schools such as the Rensselaer Polytechnic Institute: "In an age when attracting the first round intellectual draft choices from around the world is the most important competitive advantage a knowledge economy can have, why would we add barriers against such brainpower — anywhere?"[4]

Federal Reserve Chairman Ben Bernanke has made a similar observation in testimony before a congressional panel: "Our immigration laws discriminate pretty heavily against talented scientists and engineers who want to come to this country and be part of our technological establishment. By opening doors to more people with top technological skills, you'd keep companies here, and you'd have more innovation here, and you'd have more growth here."[5]

Unfortunately, the trend seems to be in precisely the opposite direction. The U.S. has never instituted a program for granting permanent residency status to foreign-born students graduating from

---

1 Florida, *Ibid.* at 100.
2 Landis, *Ibid.*
3 *Ibid.*
4 *Ibid.*
5 *Ibid.*

U.S. universities, even when those students have obtained under-graduate and graduate degrees in fields such as science, technology, and engineering, where, if allowed to stay, they would be an enormous asset to the U.S. economy. And our track record is even bleaker in terms of recruiting highly skilled immigrants that our employers want to hire. For instance, according to statistics from the Department of Homeland Security on the number of permanent green cards issued to professionals with advanced degrees, the U.S. went from issuing over 70,000 such green cards in 2008 to just over 45,000 in 2009.[1] The total number of employment-based green cards similarly went from over 165,000 in 2008 to 145,000 a year later.[2] To understand how small that number is, consider that Australia issues around 125,000 permanent residence visas every year to workers with skills critical to the economy — nearly as many as the U.S., even though the U.S. population is roughly fourteen times the size of Australia.[3]

In addition to turning away an increased number of professionals with advanced degrees, the U.S. has made it much more difficult to obtain green cards and visas across the board. Even when green cards and visas are eventually granted, the delays that occur during the process have caused major problems for U.S. corporations. One study found that visa delays alone cost U.S. businesses around $30 billion over a two-year period.[4]

Thirty billion dollars just in delays. And that number is probably growing every year, now that other countries have started deliberately targeting highly-skilled potential employees that have been caught up in the morass that constitutes the U.S. visa application process. For instance, one Canadian website states the following: "Currently on an H1B Visa or otherwise working or studying in the United States? You may be able to qualify for fast-track Canadian immigration under one of the Provincial Nomination Programs

---

1 Department of Homeland Security Office of Immigration Statistics, "Table 2: Legal Permanent Resident Flow by Major Category of Admission: Fiscal Years 2007 to 2009," http://www.dhs.gov/xlibrary/assets/statistics/publications/lpr_fr_2009.pdf.
2 DHS Office of Immigration Statistics at Table 2, *Ibid.*
3 Partnership for a New American Economy, *Ibid.* at 15.
4 Florida, *Ibid.* at 13.

(PNP) or under the Federal Skilled Worker category of Canadian immigration."[1] Whatever one's views are regarding immigration generally, no one can argue in favor of a system that has inefficiencies that cost our corporations tens of billions of dollars every year and that allow corporations from other countries to steal the highly skilled employees that our corporations want to hire.

A *New York Times* article noted that the Department of Homeland Security has developed a reputation in recent years as having a "culture of no."[2] For instance, even the most renowned foreign performing artists are having trouble getting visas for shows that have been booked in the U.S. The application process has become so arduous, expensive, and time-consuming (with delays that at times make the visa useless even if it is granted, since the date of the scheduled performance has already passed) that a number of performing artists have simply given up and taken their business elsewhere.[3] Between 2006 and 2010, the number of requests made for standard foreign performer's visas decreased by nearly 25%.[4] Artists are simply choosing to perform in other countries rather than deal with an increasingly difficult and scrutinizing visa process.

The decrease in standard foreign performer's visas is indicative of decreases across all categories of nonimmigrant visas over the last decade. In 2001, the U.S. issued over 7.5 million nonimmigrant visas, mostly for travel purposes, but also for conducting business, working, studying, performance arts, and other reasons.[5] Just two years later, that number was under 5 million.[6] Although the U.S. has been trending upward in its issuance of nonimmigrant visas since 2003, we were still only at 6.5 million in 2010.[7]

---

1 Partnership for a New American Economy, *Ibid.* at 19-20.
2 Rohter, Larry, *"U.S. Visa Rules Deprive Stages of Performers,"* The New York Times (April 11, 2012).
3 Rohter. *Ibid.*
4 *Ibid.*
5 Batalova, Jeanne & Lee, Alicia, *"Frequently Requested Statistics on Immigrants and Immigration in the United States,"* Migration Information Source (March 2012), http://www.migrationinformation.org/feature/display.cfm?ID=818 .
6 Batalova & Lee, *Ibid.*
7 *Ibid.*

Many other aspects of the U.S. economy are suffering from these restrictive immigration policies. For instance, a number of large U.S.-based corporations have chosen to hold business conferences in other countries so that foreign travelers will not have to deal with trying to get visas to travel to the U.S.[1] Scientific and techno-logical conferences are also being moved overseas to avoid forcing attendees through the U.S. visa process.[2] Each time a conference is held in another country, the U.S. economy loses out on all of the money that would have been spent on hosting that conference and its attendees. In one such documented instance, the loss of a single corporate conference to another country prevented a U.S. host city from obtaining as estimated $10 million in revenue.[3]

And in what is perhaps the biggest threat of all to the U.S. economy, some sectors appear to be suffering from an actual brain drain. In addition to losing out on a brain gain by turning away some of the best foreign-born students and by denying or delaying green cards and visas to large numbers of the exact type of highly-skilled foreign-born workers that our corporations demand, the U.S. is now having trouble holding onto the talent that is already here. Scholars have noted that "for the first time in a very long time, our very own best and brightest, established scientists, intellectu-als, and even some entrepreneurs, are starting to look elsewhere."[4] This is not surprising. As the world's best and brightest of the next generation of professionals choose to attend school and seek careers in countries that are more welcoming of them, it only makes sense that some portion of the current generation of professionals will want to follow suit.

And, just as other countries are doing everything they can to attract students that would otherwise go to U.S. universities, a number of countries are also actively taking advantage of — and exacerbating — the U.S.'s problem with a reverse brain drain. For instance, China has enacted a comprehensive program to encourage expatriates to return to China from countries such as the U.S., of-

1 Florida, *Ibid.* at 123-124.
2 *Ibid.* at 120-121.
3 *Ibid.* at 123.
4 *Ibid.* at 126.

fering signing bonuses, free housing, tax breaks, prestigious titles, and other benefits that are worth hundreds of thousands (or in some cases millions) of dollars.[1] China's program has been incredibly successful, and it has dealt a particularly harsh blow to the U.S. economy, which has supplied 55% of the highly skilled workers and entrepreneurs that China has recruited through this targeted program.[2] And who can blame these Chinese expatriates for choosing to go to a place where they are welcomed with open arms and given enormous financial and social recognition for their talents, rather than remaining in the U.S. where they would have to wend their way through an emotionally and financially draining multi-year process just to obtain the legal right to stay here permanently? While the U.S. continues to insist on imposing barriers to recruiting and retraining the highly skilled workers that our employers want and need, other countries are rolling out the red carpet.

In many ways, the argument for open borders on immigration issues is as compelling as the argument for open borders in the area of free trade.[3] While some politicians still debate the benefits of free trade, economists do not. As one scholar has put it, "for most economists, a verdict has been delivered," and the verdict is that free trade "promotes prosperity for all."[4] The basic reason is that the economy is much more efficient when it draws upon all of the resources that are available to it, regardless of where those resources are located. The same is true for the labor market. And in fact, just as economists are nearly universal in their belief in free trade, they are also nearly universal in their belief that immigrants are a net positive force on the U.S. economy.[5]

The problem is that many native-born citizens think that they can do every job as well or better than an immigrant can. Whether termed "American exceptionalism" or just plain arrogance, this mindset leads to immigration policies that pose a grave threat to the U.S. economy. The fact is that there are many jobs for which

1 Partnership for a New American Economy, *Ibid.* at 28-29.
2 *Ibid.* at 30.
3 Obhof, *Ibid.* at 164.
4 Parkin, Michael, *Macroeconomics* (5th ed. 1999) at 453.
5 Lipman, *Ibid.* at 815-817.

immigrants are better trained and more qualified, and the U.S. is handicapping itself in the global marketplace by failing to take full advantage of the highly-skilled immigrant population that is trying, but failing, to obtain entry to the U.S.

The most basic way to think of this is as simply a matter of math — while the U.S. labor force consists of over 150 million people, that is only around five percent of the worldwide labor force of over 3 billion. If you were hiring someone for a job, would you automatically throw out 19 out of every 20 applications you received without ever looking at them? If you did, how likely would you be to get the most qualified applicant? And if you failed to get the most qualified applicant, how many times could you do that before your business started losing ground to companies that looked at every job application they received?

In addition to allowing a company to hire the most qualified employees for each job, immigration is also a major cost-saver for businesses. If, for instance, a company needs to hire 100 skilled computer programmers, the company will need to pay each programmer a much higher salary if there are very few programmers to choose from.[1] By opening these positions to global competition, not only would the company be able to high better qualified applicants, but it would not have to pay them such exorbitant salaries. The end result would be a more competitive company that may even be able to allocate some of its saved resources to those employees that are paid much less than the skilled workers, which would in turn help solve some of the income inequality issues that currently plague the U.S.

A more competitive company also translates to benefits for consumers. In particular, a more efficient, well-run corporation should be able to produce goods and services of a higher quality for a cheaper price. This benefits consumers worldwide, but offers the biggest benefits to native citizens who are the most likely consumers of local products and services.

Finally, increasing the flow of skilled workers into the U.S. helps the housing sector as these new workers move into housing

---

1 Greenspan. *Ibid.*

units that would otherwise be left vacant.[1] And if they are skilled workers earning high wages, they can afford to buy the expensive houses that are least in demand during an economic recession.

There are likely many other quantifiable and unquantifiable economic benefits to bringing highly skilled immigrants to the U.S., and there is clearly no economic justification for closing our borders to them.

The Economic Impact of Shutting Out Immigrant Entrepreneurs

Perhaps the biggest impact immigrants have had — and continue to have — on the U.S. economy is through entrepreneurship. Business creation is the single greatest driver of the U.S. economy. Although the American public seems to turn a blind eye to the effect of immigration on business creation, the fact is that the U.S. economy would be nowhere near as powerful as it is today without the benefit of immigrant entrepreneurs.

Immigrants have an incredibly successful track record as entrepreneurs.[2] To begin, immigrants engage in entrepreneurial activity at rates that are roughly *double* those of native-born workers.[3] And immigrant-started businesses are more likely to succeed than those businesses started by native-born workers.[4] So much for "American exceptionalism."

The U.S. economy would have been nowhere near as successful as it has been if it were not for immigrant entrepreneurial activity. For instance, immigrants founded or co-founded around 25% of publicly-traded venture-backed companies, and nearly 50% of the top 50 venture-backed U.S. companies.[5] An immigrant or a child of an immigrant founded more than 40% of the U.S.'s Fortune 500 companies.[6] Although immigrants constitute only 12% of the U.S.

---

1 *Ibid.*
2 Weber, *Ibid.* at 776.
3 *Ibid.*
4 *Ibid.* at 777.
5 Partnership for a New American Economy, *Ibid.* at 6.
6 *Ibid.* at 1. .

population, they account for 26% of Americans who have received a Nobel Prize, as well as 24% of patent applications.[1]

It goes without saying that each successful business that an immigrant starts is a benefit to the U.S. economy. And that benefit cannot be overstated. Jobs are the first thing that comes to mind. Start-up companies are enormous job creators: in their first year of business, start-ups add roughly 3 million jobs per year to the U.S. economy.[2] One study showed that in 2006, in engineering and technology alone, there were 450,000 Americans employed by immigrant-founded U.S. corporations.[3] Just in Silicon Valley, immigrant-founded high-tech corporations have created around 70,000 jobs.[4] All of those workers had jobs because an immigrant entrepreneur created a successful company and hired them. The list of immigrant-founded or co-founded U.S. corporations includes a number of the most profitable technological companies in the world, such as Google, Intel, eBay, and Yahoo, as well as older successful corporations in other fields, including P&G, Pfizer, and U.S. Steel.

In addition to creating jobs, successful immigrant businesses add enormous revenue to U.S. coffers. One study showed that in 2006 alone, immigrant-founded or co-founded U.S. corporations contributed $52 billion in tax revenue.[5] And that is under current immigration restrictions. A more open-border policy would obviously lead to more immigrant entrepreneurship and a consequent increase in this contribution to tax revenue.

Despite the clear benefits to the U.S. economy from immigrant entrepreneurship, some claim that immigrant businesses do not help our economy. The argument is that any benefits associated with immigrant entrepreneurs are offset by the negative economic consequences resulting from displacing businesses run by native-born citizens. That zero-sum argument has been shown to be incorrect.[6] On the whole, there is no evidence that immigrant entre-

---

1 *Ibid.* at 6.
2 *Ibid.* at 10.
3 *Ibid.* at 6.
4 Florida, *Ibid.* at 107.
5 Landis, *Ibid.*
6 Weber, *Ibid.* at 792.

preneurs displace native-born businesses, and the evidence in fact shows that immigrant-founded businesses are a net benefit to the U.S. economy.[1]

***

A more open-border policy would not only reap enormous economic benefits for the U.S., but it would also be a boon to the global economy. According to some economists, if the world moved to a full open-border policy that removed all restrictions on immigration, it could lead to a doubling of global GDP.[2]

Of course, from a political standpoint, a full open-border policy is not a realistic option. But there are many steps the U.S. can take to reform our immigration policy to better suit the realities of a global economy and the global competition for talent. A recent report from the Partnership for a New American Economy notes the sharp dissonance between the current needs of the U.S. economy and the immigration policies surrounding our country's 50-year-old visa distribution system. The report makes six specific and relatively simple recommendations for reforming immigration policy to save the U.S. economy:

1. Stop sending talented foreign students with science and technology degrees home.
2. Award more green cards based on economic needs.
3. Create a visa for foreign entrepreneurs to build their firms in the U.S.
4. Let American companies hire the highly educated workers they need, where they need them.
5. Give seasonal and labor-intensive industries access to foreign workers when they cannot fill the jobs with Americans.
6. Allow local governments to recruit more immigrants to meet regional needs.[3]

These are simple steps that would go a long way toward rebuilding the U.S. economy and ensuring that we retain a competi-

---

1 *Ibid.*

2 Hamilton, Bob & Whalley, John, "Efficiency and Distributional Implications of Global Restrictions on Labour Mobility: Calculations and Policy Implications," Journal of Developmental Economics, vol. 14, pp. 61-75 (1984).at 70-72.

3 Partnership for a New American Economy, *Ibid.* at 34-35.

tive edge in the global marketplace. These reforms would help reverse the trends that are currently leading so many talented foreign-born students and workers to move to other countries rather than deal with the U.S. immigration system. If, on the other hand, we continue to erect barriers to entry, while other countries lay down red carpets, we should not be surprised to one day find that, in the global marketplace, we are the ones being left out in the cold.

In the end, the U.S. economy does not need to be saved from immigrants — it needs to be saved by them.

8. RACE AND THE SHAPING OF U.S. IMMIGRATION POLICY

Introduction

The date is October 13, 2004, some 147 years after Chief Justice Roger Taney and the infamous Dred Scott case. Representing the United States government, Deputy Solicitor General Edwin Kneedler, stands before the United States Supreme Court and tells the Court that the nation needs to protect its borders and in doing so some noncitizens must be treated as if they have no rights to due process.[1]

At issue is the ultimate fate of over 1000 persons of color, Mariel Cubans held in federal custody nearly 25 years after the boatlift. Two of the Cuban detainees have been incarcerated for 19 years. A total of 33 aliens have waited in jail for more than 15 years to be deported.

Justice Souter grills Solicitor General Kneedler about the legal "fiction" of pretending that Mariel Cubans, who have been here for a quarter-century, have no more rights than immigrants showing up at the border: "That fiction of exclusion can't be used for constitutional purposes, can it? . . . You have a due process clause that says

---

[1] Oral argument before the U.S. Supreme Court, Clark v. Martinez, 543 U. S. 371 (2005) (Oct. 13, 2004).

'persons,' not 'citizens' are entitled to constitutional protections?"
Justice John Paul Stevens continues the questioning of Kneedler by
asking, "how far the government would carry the 'no rights' argument?" "Can we kill them?" he asks.[1]

Six miles away at the local Immigration and Naturalization
Service ("INS")[2] office in Arlington, Virginia, things are not much
better:

> "Dante would have been delighted by the Immigration and Nat-
> uralization Service waiting rooms. They would have provided
> him with a tenth Circle of Hell. There is something distinctly
> infernal about the spectacle of so many lost souls waiting
> around so hopelessly, mutually incomprehensible in virtually
> every language under the sun, each clutching a number from
> one of those ticket-issuing machines which may or may not be
> honored by the INS clerks before the end of the civil service
> working day.... [These] huddled masses accept this treatment
> with a horrible passivity. Perhaps it is imbued in them by eons
> of arbitrary government in their native lands. Only rarely is
> there a flurry of protest."[3]

Only a mile or so away from the Supreme Court, the House of
Representatives — led by a hard-line Republican majority — has
just passed its version of the 2006 immigration bill, the Border Protection, Antiterrorism, and Illegal Immigration Reform Act of 2005
(H.R. 4437). The bill is all about enforcement and building fences,
and it is silent on the issue of legalization of the estimated 12 million
illegal aliens in the United States. The bill would make visitors to
the United States who overstay their visas (currently a civil offense)
even by a day, felons, subject to federal prosecution. An amendment
to reduce the crime of over-staying to a misdemeanor was defeated.
And seven million employers would be required to submit social
security numbers and other information to a national database to
verify the legal status of workers.

So now we have the imagery. Why the organized assault on immigrants? Could it be because they are largely persons of color? Is

---

1 *Id.*

2 Now the U.S. Citizenship and Immigration Services (USCIS).

3 Peter Brimelow, *Time to Rethink Immigration?*, NAT'L REV. (June 22, 1992), *available* at
http://www.vdare.com/pb/time to rethink.htm.

it anti-immigrant fervor or racist fervor or both? In order to probe these questions, one must recognize that the current assault on immigrant rights can only be explained by understanding the fundamental weaknesses in the underpinnings of support for immigrant rights and causes. In particular, one must understand the following factors, all of which have played — and continue to play — a large role in the formation of U.S. immigration policy:

1. The U.S. has provided no fundamental constitutional protection for immigrants, which has fostered blind judicial deference to administrative agency decisions against immigrants and judicial indifference to the rights of aliens.
2. Many U.S. immigration policies have been crafted and administered by white Anglo-Saxon supremacists.
3. The U.S. provided no due process rights for aliens until the twentieth century.
4. White Americans have created a culture of racial superiority that existed for hundreds of years from 1789 until 1965 and beyond.[1]

When one examines the composition of immigrants, both legal and illegal, in the 1990s, the numbers are telling. And one point is clear: one cannot separate race from the shaping of U.S. immigration policy.[2] Professor Lucas Guttentag has noted that the U.S. has a "legacy of racism," and "immigration law and policy cannot be divorced from issues of race, national origin, ethnicity, and color."[3] Indeed, U.S. immigration policy has a history that "is steeped in race and racism."[4] Historically, "the U.S. government [has] commonly [gone] to extraordinary lengths to halt feared mass migrations of people of color."[5]

---

1 Rogers M. Smith, CIVIC IDEALS: CONFLICTING VISIONS OF CITIZENSHIP IN U.S. HISTORY 17 (Yale Univ. Press 1997); see also Gerald L. Neuman, Strangers to the Constitution: Immigrants, Borders, and Fundamental Law (Princeton Univ. Press 1996).

2 E.g., Lucas Guttentag, Immigration Reform: A Civil Rights Issue, 3 STAN. J. CIV. RTS. & CIV. LIBERTIES 157, 158 (2007).

3 Id.

4 Id.; see also Brian G. Slocum, Canons, The Plenary Power Doctrine, and Immigration Law, 34 Fla. St. U. L. Rev. 363, 407 (2007) ("The federal government's early restrictions on immigration were motivated by racial animus . . . .").

5 Kevin R. Johnson, "THE 'HUDDLED MASSES' MYTH": IMMIGRATION AND CIVIL RIGHTS 40 (Temple Univ. Press 2004).

A look at the actual immigration numbers during the 1990s reveals the strong connection between immigration and race. Between 1991 and 2000, 9.1 million legal immigrants arrived in the United States.[1] The following chart provides a breakdown of the origins of these 9.1 legal immigrants:
FIGURE 1[2]

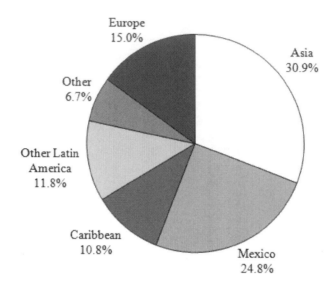

As this chart shows, of these legal immigrants, roughly 25% were from Mexico, 31% from Asia, 11% from the Caribbean, and 12% from the rest of Latin America.[3] Of the remaining 21% from Eu-

---

1 U.S. Dep't of Homeland Sec., Office of Immigration Statistics, *2003 Yearbook of Immigration Statistics*, at 14 (Sept. 2004), *available at* http://www.dhs.gov/ximgtn/statistics/publications/YrBk03Im.shtm.

2 *Ibid.*

3 U.S. INS, *Estimates of the Unauthorized Immigrant Population Residing in the United States: 1990 to 2000*, at 1 (Jan. 31, 2003), *available at* http://www.dhs.gov/xlibrary/assets/statistics/publications/Ill_Report_1211.pdf.

rope and other countries, it is likely that a significant proportion of those persons were persons of colors, particularly considering the high numbers of East Indian, Caribbean, and Arab immigration to Europe and elsewhere. In sum, better than 90% of the legal immigrants who immigrated to the United States in the previous decade were persons of color.

In that same decade, 1991-2000, the number of illegal immigrants residing in the United States rose to 7 million. The following chart provides a breakdown of the estimated origins of these 7 million illegal immigrants:

FIGURE 2[1]

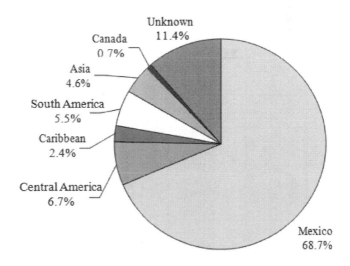

As this chart shows, in this category, the predominance of the Americas is even greater: roughly 69% of the entire total 7 million undocumented immigrants were from Mexico, 12% were from the rest of Latin America, and 2% were from the Caribbean.[2] Again, an

---

1 See *Id.*
2 *See id.*

overwhelming number of immigrants during this time period were persons of color.

To better explore and understand these questions about race and the shaping of U.S. immigration policy, this Article examines these and other issues as follows. Part I describes the "white supremacist" order model of Professors Desmond King and Rogers Smith — a model that explains some of the racial underpinnings in immigration law. Part II provides a brief historiography of the origins of the major immigration statutes and policies underpinning the development of the "white supremacist" order as applied to immigration policy. Part III analyzes and dispels the notion that the 1965 Immigration Act's removal of national origins quotas effectively removed most aspects of "racial" selection or color in immigration preferences, and further argues that race continues to shape our immigration policies. Part IV describes some of the ways that color-based discrimination against immigrants is harmful not only to immigrants, but also to the entire U.S. and our economy, which is currently dependent in many ways on an influx of foreign talent — talent that is increasingly headed elsewhere. Finally, this Article concludes with a brief exploration of some of the ways that we could change U.S. immigration policy to work toward eliminating the vestiges of racism that currently prevail.

I. The King and Smith Model

For the purposes of this paper, this Article will accept and apply the "white supremacist" order model delineated by Desmond King and Rogers Smith.[1] That model argues that "American politics has historically been constituted in part by two evolving but linked 'racial institutional orders': a set of 'white supremacist' orders and a competing set of 'transformative egalitarian' orders."[2] This thesis rejects the idea that racial injustices are regrettable deviations from American traditions that generally tolerate other

---

1 *See generally* Desmond S. King and Rogers M. Smith, *Racial Orders in American Political Development*, 99 AM. POL. SCI. REV. 75, 75-89 (2005).
2 *Id.* at 75.

cultures.[1]According to Professors King and Smith, the nation has actually "been pervasively constituted by systems of racial hierarchy since its inception."[2] They summarize their thesis as follows:

> To sketch the argument developed here: at the nation's founding, a political coalition of Americans formed that gained sufficient power to direct most governing institutions, and also economic, legal, educational, residential, and social institutions, in ways that established a hierarchical order of white supremacy, though never without variations, inconsistencies, and resistance.[3]

This framework challenges the "strong tendency in American political development literature, tracing to Louis Hartz (1955), to theorize racial issues as ultimately products of the antebellum 'master/slave' order."[4]

The Tocquevillian and Hartz liberal America paradigms are largely deficient because those traditions were meant to be shared only by white men, largely of northern European descent: "White northern Europeans thought themselves superior, culturally and probably biologically, to Africans, Native American Indians, and all other races and civilizations."[5] Indeed, in the earlier part of the twentieth century, "[r]acial and ethnic stereotyping and eugenics were popularly discussed as an exact science."[6] Prominent scholars "called for 'Nordic supremacy,'" and one key congressional leader "complained about the 'mongrelizing' effect the new immigration had on American society."[7] Only those who were "100 percent American" — which at the time referred to white Anglo-Saxons

---

1 See, e.g., Kevin R. Johnson, *OPENING THE FLOODGATES: WHY AMERICA NEEDS TO RETHINK ITS BORDERS AND IMMIGRATION LAW S* 20 (New York Univ. Press 2007) (emphasis added) ("Most Americans, for example, today look with shame at the exclusion of Chinese immigrants in the late 1800s and of southern and eastern Europeans, including many Jews, in the early twentieth century. Mass deportations of Mexican immigrants throughout the twentieth century . . . are *blemishes on this nation's proud history."*).

2 See King et al., *supra* note 16, at 75.

3 *Id.* at 77

4 *Id* at 79

5 See Smith, *supra* note 5, at 17

6 Bill Ong Hing, *DEFINING AMERICA THROUGH IMMIGRATION POLICY* 54 (Temple Univ. Press 2004).

7 *Id.*

and other "pure Caucasians" — were free from the attacks spurred by this renewed nativism.[1]

The assault on immigration can take two broad forms. The first and most blatant instance is legislation (such as the Chinese Exclusion Laws) which singles out persons from specific countries. These laws often "encod[ed] racial prerequisites to citizenship according to the familiar black-white categories of American race relations."[2] The second instance is a class view of immigrants of all kinds and races as a lower form of humanity when viewed by white Anglo-Saxon males.

The King & Smith model can and has been applied specifically to immigration.[3] Immigration policy was shaped by the dominant thinking of white Anglo-Saxon Protestant male superiority: "Until the 1920s, southern and eastern Europeans could immigrate and be naturalized without limit. From then until 1965, their numbers were limited explicitly because lawmakers now viewed them, too, as 'lower races.'"[4] As a result, "from the 1882 Chinese Exclusion Act, through the Johnson-Reed 1924 Immigration Act . . . to the Immigration and Naturalization Act of 1952 affirming racial discrimination, domestic racial institutions and their proponents have interacted profoundly with immigration policy."[5] Their model seeks to highlight how the southern and western alliance linked immigra-

---

1 *Id.*

2 Mae M. Ngai, *IMPOSSIBLE SUBJECTS: ILLEGAL ALIENS AND THE MAKING OF MODERN AMERICA* 38 (Princeton Univ. Press 2004).

3 For an interesting description of general societal acceptance of discrimination in immigration policy see Catherine Dauvergne. *"Citizenship with a Vengeance"* 8 *Theoretical Inquiries L.* 489, 494-95 (2007) ("Migration laws aim to discriminate — to determine who will be admitted and who will be excluded. . . . The underlying assumption of the immigration preferences of prosperous Western nations is that liberal nations are generally morally justified in closing their borders. That is, the discrimination inherent in this law is justified by the need of the liberal community for closure and its right to identity. Racist provisions eventually came to be seen as abhorrent to liberal principle, but the basic logic of a migration law which discriminates between applicants on the basis of choosing those who best meet the needs and values of the nation has not been impugned. The criteria that immigration laws enshrine read as a code of national values, determining who some "we" group will accept as potential future members. . . . The bodies for whom these answers are a fit can pass through this filter and become formal legal citizens.")

4 *See* Smith, *supra* note 5, at 17.

5 *See* King et al., *supra* note 16, at 75, 88.

tion and segregation into a more potent white supremacist order, as demonstrated by the new political alliances in those regions.[1]

And lastly, the King & Smith model has been applied to the federal bureaucracy: "[F]ederal departments helped to devise, implement, and monitor the segregationist order legally in place between 1896 and 1954."[2] I argue that this racial order has been transformed from the segregationist slavery order to a federal bureaucracy racial order that is all but too visible in its effect and application to immigrants, who are persons primarily of color.

II. The Origins of U.S. Immigration Policy

The American Constitution was remarkably silent on the subject of immigration and citizenship:

> The 1787 text mentioned citizenship three times as a requirement for federal offices, though only the elective ones. It gave Congress the power to establish a uniform rule of naturalization. It also referred to citizenship in assigning jurisdiction to the federal courts . . . . But the Constitution did not define or describe citizenship, discuss criteria for inclusion or exclusion, or address the sensitive relationship between state and national citizenship.[3]

The great constitutional historian Alexander Bickel wrote that "the concept of citizenship plays only the most minimal role in the American constitutional scheme."[4] In truth, the Constitution said little about citizenship, even though it was of pivotal — not minimal — importance.[5] And despite America's receptivity to brilliant immigrants, courts have long denied immigrants rights not explicitly protected by provisions in the U.S. constitution. For instance, "one strategy for silencing objections to government policy has

---

1 *See id.* ("It is doubtful that the prorestriction immigration regime, initiated in 1882 and in place until 1965, could have existed without a white supremacist alliance in Congress of southern Democrats and western Republicans, a coalition that provided successive chairs of the two houses' Immigration Committees. They gained further reinforcement from northeastern nativist elites. These "strange bedfellow" alliances show that the racial order promoted linkages across diverse political groupings that, in turn, helped maintain that order.").

2 *Id.* at 85.

3 See Smith, *supra* note 5, at 115.

4 Alexander M. Bickel, *THE MORALITY OF CONSENT* 33 (Yale Univ. Press 1975).

5 *See id.* at 36.

---

been to deny that the Constitution affords any protection to the objector."[1]

Eventually, the courts recognized that aliens had due process rights,[2] but too often relaxed or ignored those rights on the grounds of national emergency or compelling national interest.[3] As one scholar has noted, "[u]nder traditional immigration law, the government is afforded free reign to treat noncitizens, denominated 'aliens,' as it sees fit."[4] This situation stands in stark contrast with U.S. citizens, who enjoy rights that (at least in theory) "generally cannot lawfully be revoked."[5]

The first law related to immigration was the Immigration Act of 1790, which restricted naturalized citizenship to "whites." Mainstream immigration literature generally avers that immigration to America in the nineteenth century was largely open, without regard to race or restrictions on numerical limitations.[6] Granted, there was

---

1 Gerald L. Neuman, *STRANGERS TO THE CONSTITUTION: IMMIGRANTS, BORDERS, AND FUNDAMENTAL LAW* 3 (Princeton Univ. Press 1996).

2 *See, e.g., id.* at 4 ("The Supreme Court has also held for more than a century that aliens within the United States are persons entitled to constitutional protection."). Professor Neuman was referring to *Yick Wo v. Hopkins*, 118 U.S. 356 (1886), and *Wong Wing v. United States*, 163 U.S. 228 (1896), and he notes that the "Court had never suggested a contrary holding before" these two cases. *See id.* at 191.

3 The aftermath of September 11 has provided numerous examples of significant restrictions on alien rights. *See, e.g.,* HING, *supra* note 23, at 268 ("In some situations, the Bush administration attempted to bypass certain processes by imposing 'military justice.' The president asserted the authority to hold people in military custody incommunicado, without any individualized hearing into the basis for their detention, without access to a lawyer, and without judicial review. He set up military tribunals in which detainees could be tried, and ultimately executed, without independent judicial review and without anyone outside the military, including the defendant, ever seeing the evidence on which the conviction rested."); *see also* Johnson, *OPENING THE FLOODGATES, supra* note 18, at 32 ("Unfortunately, the 'war on terror' has been used to rationalize a wide variety of aggressive policies that have had little to do with national security and public safety. For example, in the name of fighting terrorism, the Department of Justice announced that it would begin enforcing a rule allowing for the deportation of immigrants who fail to report their change of address within ten days.").

4 Johnson, "THE 'HUDDLED MASSES' MYTH," *supra* note 9, at 3.

5 *Id.* at 4. Of course, the word "lawfully" does some work here. Although American history is rife with instances of the government ignoring the rights of citizens, the point here is that such actions are not lawful. In the immigration context, on the other hand, when the same actions are taken against immigrants, the law often has nothing to say on the matter. *See id.* at 3-4.

6 *See, e.g.,* Daniel J. Tichenor, *DIVIDING LINES: THE POLITICS OF IMMIGRATION CONTROL IN AMERICA* 2 (Princeton Univ. Press 2002) ("Save for the fleeting

no federal control over immigration until 1891, when immigration technically became the province of the federal government by the creation of the Office of Immigration Control, under the auspices of the U.S. Treasury Department.[1] Also, there "was no formal Border Patrol until 1924."[2] Nevertheless, the concept that America enjoyed "open borders" from 1789 until the 1924 National Origins Act may be severely overstated.[3] According to one scholar, state and local governments have always regulated the movement of people across legal borders through the use of criminal laws, vagrancy laws, quarantine laws, registration laws, and (before 1865) the law of slavery.[4]

That being said, the 1882 enactment of the Chinese Exclusion Act, which prevented Chinese immigration for sixty years, heralded the first major legislatively based racial attack on immigrants. This law was undoubtedly the result of fears that had been "inflamed by racism."[5] It marked the legislative naissance of "the undesirable Asian" mentality in the United States.[6] The act was brought on by a xenophobic panic and hysteria surrounding large amounts of Chinese laborers imported to build the railways and work in the mines.[7] It was followed by amendments in 1885 and 1887 banning the trade in contract labor and thereby "prohibiting anyone from prepaying an immigrant's transportation to the United States in return for a promise to provide service."[8]

Leading up to the Chinese Exclusion Act, the Chinese were the first to enter the United States in large numbers:

Alien and Sedition Acts, the national government embraced an essentially laissez-faire approach to immigration for many decades after the founding."); *see also* Neuman, *supra* note 35, at 19 (noting that legal discussions often rest upon the "myth . . . that the borders of the United States were legally open" during this time").

1 Neuman, *supra* note 35, at 19.

2 Roger Daniels, *GUARDING THE GOLDEN DOOR: AMERICAN IMMIGRATION POLICY AND IMMIGRANTS SINCE 1882,* 237 (Hill and Wang, 2004).

3 Neuman, *supra* note 35, at 19.

4 *Id.* at 19-43.

5 Johnson, *OPENING THE FLOODGATES, supra* note 18, at 23.

6 For a thorough explanation of the rise of "the undesirable Asian" mentality, *see generally* Hing, *supra* note 23, at 28-50.

7 *See, e.g., id.* at 37 ("By 1982, . . . most public sentiment now favored exclusion . . . ."); *id.* at 38 (noting that Congress passed the Chinese Exclusion Act in response to "xenophobic national clamor").

8 *Id.* at 121.

Driven by the rice shortage and devastation of the Taiping Rebellion and drawn by the lure of gold, Chinese peasants and laborers began making the long journey in the 1840s. As the population of China increased dramatically from 275 million in 1779 to 430 million in 1850, rice became scarce . . . . With the cession of Hong Kong to Britain . . . in 1842, southeastern China was for the first time open to travelers and trade with the West.[1]

The Chinese were at first officially welcomed in the United States.[2] The 1848 discovery of gold "led to a growing demand for a ready supply of Chinese labor."[3] American industries actively recruited Chinese to work on railroad construction, mining, and other activities, and in 1852 "the governor of California even recommended a system of land grants to induce the immigration and settlement of Chinese.[4] As a result, by 1882, roughly 300,000 Chinese had entered the U.S., and many of them remained to work in California and other western states.[5] Soon, however, groups — particularly labor groups that felt threatened by the new influx of immigrants — began to organize a strong resistance movement that ultimately led to the Chinese Exclusion Act.[6]

Around 1905, the assault on Asians shifted from Chinese to Japanese.[7] In 1907, a "gentlemen's agreement" between President Theodore Roosevelt and the Government of Japan curtailed Japanese immigration to the United States.[8] Unfavorable sentiment toward the Japanese had begun to grow at the turn of the century as they began migrating to the western United States.[9] Originally, Japanese had come to Hawaii to satisfy agricultural labor demands; however, after "Hawaii was annexed in 1898, the Japanese were able to use it

---

1 *Id.* at 28.
2 *Id.* at 29.
3 *Id.*
4 *Id.*
5 *Id.*
6 *Id.* at 30-40.
7 *Id.* at 42.
8 *Id.*
9 *Id.* at 41.

as a stepping stone to the [U.S.] mainland[,] . . . [and] [e]conomic competition with white farm workers soon erupted."[1]

The 1917 Literacy Law is another important example of the "who-is-a real-American" enactments that have historically played a major role in U.S. immigration policy.[2] The Immigration Act of 1917 required all aliens who were both over the age of sixteen and were physically capable of reading to be able to read English or some other language or dialect. One scholar has noted that "[t]he history of the immigration literacy requirement finds its origins in the nativism that was directed at southern and eastern Europeans who dominated the numbers of immigrants to the United States at the turn of the century."[3] At the time, "opponents of immigration noted with dread that the national origins of most newcomers to the United States were shifting steadily from northern and western to southern and eastern European sources,"[4] and southern and eastern Europeans were not seen as "true Americans."[5] In efforts that were remarkably similar to those used to exclude Chinese immigrants, nativists claimed to have "expert findings . . . that portrayed southern and eastern Europeans as racially inferior."[6] The nationalist outlook viewed "a homogenous population as the foundation of a strong state."[7]

The Quota Law of 1921, enacted as a "temporary" measure, introduced for the first time numerical limitations on immigration.[8] With certain exceptions, an annual ceiling of 350,000 was set alongside a new nationality quota limiting admissions to 3% of each national-

---

1 *Id.*

2 *Id.* at 50.

3 *Id.*

4 Tichenor, *supra*, note 40, at 12

5 Hing, *supra*, note23, at 50

6 Tichenor, *supra* note 40, at 12; *accord* Hing, *supra* note 23, at 61 (emphasis added) ("The history of the efforts that led to the enactment of the 1917 literacy law makes it clear that southern and eastern Europeans, particularly Jews and Italians, were not welcomed as Americans by much of the polity. The eugenics movement was in full swing, and *racial distinctions were now placed on a scientific hierarchy* with those of Nordic descent (i.e., western Europeans) at the zenith. Now, barring certain races from intermingling was not only socially desirable but also scientifically appropriate.").

7 Tichenor, *supra* note 40, at 10.

8 *E.g.*, Hing, *supra* note 23, at 68.

ity's group representation based upon the 1910 census.[1] The law was designed to stem the flow of immigrants coming from southern and eastern Europe.[2] It also contained restrictions that were "overtly anti-Semitic," and Albert Johnson, who was the Chairman of the House Committee on Immigration at the time, even went so far as to call Jews "filthy" and "unAmerican" in his efforts to persuade others that quotas were needed to prevent an influx of Jews.[3]

In 1924, Congress enacted the now famous National Origins Act, which further reduced the annual ceiling on immigration to 150,000 and further reduced per country nationality immigration to 2%.[4] The law adopted a national origins formula that was based on the number of foreign-born persons of each national origin in the United States in 1890, which, as one scholar notes, predated "the major wave of southern and eastern European immigrants."[5] A House report explicitly stated that these measures were racially based: "[The quota system] is used in an effort to preserve, as nearly as possible, the racial status quo in the United States. It is hoped to guarantee, as best we can at this late date, racial homogeneity."[6] Just as prominent scientists and academics supported the racial superiority model that led to the 1917 Literacy Law, the National Origins Act enjoyed similar support:

> As one commentator remarked approvingly in 1924, the national origins quota system was "a scientific plan for keeping America American." Implicit in such rationale, or course, was the view that persons of northern European stock were superior to members of other groups. . . . The racial hierarchy endorsed by proponents of the national origins quota system

---

1 *Id.*

2 *See, e.g.,* Daniels, *supra* note 42, at 48 ((noting that the Senator who introduced the bill was "clearly aim[ing] at reducing immigration from Eastern and Southern Europe"); *see also* Hing, *supra* note 23, at 68 ("Since most of those living in the Unites States in 1910 were northern or western European, the quota for southern and eastern Europeans was smaller . . . .").

3 Daniels, *supra* note 42, at 47-48.

4 *E.g.,* Hing, *supra* note 23, at 68-69.

5 *Id.* at 68.

6 Johnson, *THE "HUDDLED MASSES" MYTH, supra* note 9, at 23 (emphasis removed) (citing STAFF OF HOUSE COMM. ON IMMIGRATION AND NATURALIZATION, REPORT ON RESTRICTION OF IMMIGRATION, H.R. REP. NO. 68-350, pt. 1, at 16 (1924)).

---

was entirely consistent with the academic literature of the day, which viewed the "races" of southern and eastern Europe as inferior to those of northern Europe.[1]

The 1924 law further provided that there would be a new quota beginning in 1929. Professor Bill Ong Hing noted the ways in which the new quota perpetuated racial biases that favored white society:

> The national origins formula used the ethnic background of the entire U.S. population, rather than the first-generation immigration population, as its base for calculating national quotas. Because the U.S. population was still predominantly Anglo-Saxon, the national origins quota restricted the newer immigrant groups more severely than the foreign-born formula of the previous quota laws. The national origins quota allotted 85 percent of the total 150,000 [immigrants] to countries from northern and western Europe, while southern and eastern countries received only the remaining 15 percent of the total.[2]

These efforts met the goals they set out to achieve, and the U.S. experienced a major decline in the amount of immigrants coming from southern and Eastern Europe.[3]

The passage of the 1952 Immigration Act confirmed quotas based on national origins.[4] But the Act went much further: "Influenced by the cold war atmosphere and anticommunist fervor of the post-World War II era and the onset of the Korean War, . . . [t]he 1952 law was more direct and reminiscent of the Alien and Sedition Laws of early America: individuals who held certain political viewpoints were not welcome [as] those viewpoints were deemed un-American."[5] "Subversives" and communists were specifically excluded for eligibility, as were gays and lesbians.[6] Indeed, the 1952

---

1 *Id.* (citations omitted).

2 Hing, *supra* note 23, at 69.

3 *Id.* at 68-70.

4 *E.g., id.* at 74 (citing President Truman's veto message) ("The bill would continue, practically without change, the national origins quota system, which was enacted into law in 1924.").

5 *Id.* at 73-74.

6 *See generally id.* at 73-92; The use of immigration laws to discriminate against homosexuals has a long history in the United States. *See, e.g.,* Johnson, *OPENING THE FLOODGATES, supra* note 18, at 235 n.16 ("Along these lines, the U.S. immigration laws historically have regulated sexuality by denying entry into the country of gays and lesbians."); Smith, *supra* note 5, at 22-23 ("[H]omosexuals .

law led to nearly forty years of explicit exclusion of the immigration of homosexuals,[1] followed by various aspects of U.S. immigration policy that continue to have disparate impacts on this group of individuals.[2]

In sum, the 1952 Act "was not just about perpetuating old exclusion regimes directed at Asians, Jews, Catholics, and southern and eastern Europeans."[3] Now, persons whose political opinions or sexual identities did not fit within the American model were added to the list of undesirables. Professor Albert Memmi, a preeminent scholar on racism, has noted that racism is in many ways an expression of ethnophobia, or, more generally, "'heterophobia,' which covers all forms of domination based on real or imaginary differences between groups: men and women, gays and straights, natives and immigrants, and so on."[4]

III. The 1965 Act and Beyond: Vestiges of Color-Based Discrimination Remain

The 1965 Immigration Act technically abolished the national origins quota system and statutory vestiges of Asian exclusion laws.[5] The Act placed a 20,000 annual limit on immigration for persons from any single country. However, the Act established an overall limit of 120,000 immigrants from the Western Hemisphere. As a result, "[a]lthough the rest of the world enjoyed an expansion in numerical limitations after 1965, Mexico and the Western Hemisphere for the first time were suddenly faced with numerical restrictions."[6]

The 1965 Act was "sold" as the piece of legislation that would end national-origin-based quotas and thereby help end discrimination of persons of color in the United States. Shortly after the law was passed, it became apparent that it would have the opposite im-

---

. . .had [long ago] become explicit targets of discrimination in American citizenship laws.").

1 Johnson, THE "HUDDLED MASSES" MYTH, *supra* note 9, at 140.

2 *Id.* at 141, 145-51.

3 Hing, *supra* note 23, at 91.

4 Kwame Anthony Appiah, Foreword, *in* Albert Memmi, *RACISM* ix (Steve Martinot trans., Univ. of Minnesota Press 1999).

5 *See, e.g.,* Hing, *supra* note 23, at 95 ("President Kennedy's hopes for abolishing the quota system were realized when the 1965 amendments were enacted.").

6 *Id.*

pact. Specifically, persons from Mexico, Hong Kong, India, and the Philippines quickly exceeded the 20,000 per country limitation and began to experience horrendous backlogs in visa quota availability — some as long as 10-15 year waits:

> Even though [since 1965] the law is colorblind on its face, the modern U.S. immigration laws continue to have discriminatory impacts. People of color from the developing world, especially those from nations that send relatively large numbers of immigrants to the Unites States, are the most disadvantaged of all groups, especially those of a select few high-immigration nations. They suffer disproportionately from tighter entry requirements and heightened immigration enforcement. For example, under certain visa categories, many citizens from India, the Philippines, and Mexico face much longer waits for entry into the United States than similarly situated noncitizens from other nations.[1]

Cases involving immigrants from Hong Kong are particularly striking. Because Hong Kong was a British Crown Colony, it was allocated only 5,000 visas per annum under U.S. law.[2] In the twenty year period leading up to the July 1, 1997 handover of Hong Kong to the People's Republic of China, Hong Kong nationals who carried limited British passports began to look for places to immigrate in view of the looming change in sovereignty.[3] Because of the paltry 5,000 per annum visa limitation in the United States, Hong Kong nationals faced waiting times as long as 15 years for a visa to the United States.[4] Since this was an obviously unacceptable option, they began to look to other countries, such as Canada, for immigration options. As a result, over 500,000 Hong Kong nationals immigrated to Canada between 1977 and 1997. During that same period, the United States never seriously considered increasing the Hong

---

1 Johnson, *OPENING THE FLOODGATES*, *supra* note 18, at 51.

2 E.g., Carolyn Waller & Linda M. Hoffman, "United States Immigration Law as a Foreign Policy Tool: The Beijing Crisis and the United States Response," 3 GEO. IMMIGR. L.J. 313, 352 (1989).

3 *E.g., id.* at 351 (referring to the "issue of existing Hong Kong nationals anxious to leave the British Crown Colony before reversion to the PRC in 1997").

4 E.g., Jesse I. Santana, "The Proverbial Catch-22: The Unconstitutionality of Section Five of the Immigration Marriage Fraud Amendments of 1986," 25 CAL. W. L. REV. 1, 2 n.4 (1989).

Kong quota to the regular 20,000 per country limitation. As a result, the United States lost out on Hong Kong immigrants and investors.[1]

In addition, the 1965 Act for the first time put in place a national Alien Labor Certification system. Under this system, workers who sought visas through skills or occupations were required to obtain a certification from the U.S. Department of Labor that their employment in the United States would not displace or negatively affect a U.S. worker. That system ultimately proved to be complicated, slow, and burdensome, and it reduced the number of employment-based workers who would have otherwise been eligible for a U.S. visa.

By 1976, the assault on foreign medical graduates reached peak levels. Foreign medical graduates ("FMGs") were recruited by U.S. residency training programs for one principal reason — there were not enough U.S. medical graduates to fill all of the residency slots in the U.S., and the FMGs, many of whom had been doctors in their native countries for at least ten years, were a cheap source of labor. Nevertheless, Congress came to a contrary conclusion and passed the Health Professions Educational Assistance Act of 1976 to try to limit the amount of FMGs. [2]

The assault on FMGs came in two ways. First, the J-1 or Exchange Visitor Visa program was introduced. The program allowed FMGs to come to the United States on temporary J-1 visas to work in hospitals as medical residents and upon the completion

---

1 Even specific efforts to increase investment from Hong Kong immigrants have not alleviated this problem, and the Canadian economy has continued to benefit from investments that never make their way into the U.S. See, e.g., Robert C. Groven, Note, "Setting Our Sights: The United States and Canadian Investor Visa Programs," 4 MINN. J. GLOBAL TRADE 271, 272 (1995) (noting that the U.S. Investor Visa program has "floundered, while the Canadian program continues to draw large numbers of cash-laden immigrants"). For a discussion of some of the other ways in which U.S. immigration policy has had a detrimental effect on the American economy, see infra Part IV.

2 See, e.g., Hing, supra note 23, at 96 (noting that when Congress passed the Act, it declared "that there was no longer a shortage of physicians and surgeons in the United States and that no further need existed for the admission of aliens to fill those positions"). Professor Hing goes on to note that in reality "FMGs were providing a critical service throughout the United States," and that the efforts behind the 1976 Act were reminiscent of efforts to exclude "the competition felt by white workers when Chinese, Japanese, and Asian Indian immigrant workers arrived in the United States from 1850 to 1917." Id.

thereof receive certification of residency training requirements in their respective medical specialties. There was one catch, however, and that was the two year foreign residency requirement listed in § 212(e) of the Immigration and Nationality Act, which required FMGs, after completion of their residencies, to return to their native countries for two years. Basically, our law said that now that we the United States have availed ourselves of your services, you must go home. After departing the U.S. and returning to their home countries to serve out the two year foreign residence requirement, many of the FMGs who sought to return to the U.S. found hostile officers at U.S. embassies. These officers refused to issue any kind of visa to the would-be returning FMGs.

The second primary assault on FMGs came with the imposition of the Visa Qualifying Exam ("VQE"). The VQE was designed to stem the flow of FMGs. Spearheaded by Senator Ted Kennedy, the restrictions were seen as a way to ration healthcare. The idea was that if fewer doctors are available, wait times to see a doctor would increase and patients who now must wait weeks to see a doctor might either be well or no longer interested in seeing a physician when facing weeks of wait time.

The VQE also had a distinct racial component. The exam included a basic science component and an English skills portion. Physicians from Asia and Mexico, in particular, had extreme difficulty in passing the exam since their basic education was not conducted in English. Contrast this to doctors from the U.K., who had a much easier time with the exam. The exam was extremely unfair in one other respect. Many FMGs already in the U.S. possessed valid state licenses to practice medicine and were in the process of acquiring permanent residence status in the United States. The imposition of the VQE was an immigration requirement, not a licensure requirement. Hence, doctors who possessed valid state licenses and who were already practicing medicine were now faced with the immigration requirement of passing the new VQE, since otherwise they would not be eligible to become permanent residents.

By 1986, the surge in Latino and Asian immigration became significant.[1] Congress, reflecting uneasy sentiments about the rising levels of these immigrants, introduced what was known as "diversity" visas:

> Although the country's population was still overwhelmingly white and of European descent, Congress added a little-publicized provision in the Immigration and Reform and Control Act to help thirty-six countries that had been "adversely affected" by the 1965 changes. To be considered "adversely affected," a country must have been issued fewer visas after 1965 than before. Thus, the list included such countries as Great Britain, Germany, and France, but no countries from Africa, which had sent few immigrants prior to 1965. [2]

Thus, the diversity program was not about diversity at all; rather, it was a carefully crafted piece of legislation designed to favor white applicants over persons of color.[3]

The new allocations under the diversity visa program were significant. Fifteen thousand visas were made available in addition to the 20,000 per country limitation. Persons qualifying for such visas needed no close family relatives in the United States or any special skills or advanced education.[4] A high school diploma was enough, and applicants merely needed to send in a simple application to be selected from the diversity lottery.[5]

Four years after the introduction of "diversity" visas, Congress passed the Immigration Act of 1990. While legal immigration continued to be dominated by Asians and Latinos even after the enactment of the diversity lottery program, Congress was apparently intent on reducing Asian and Latino immigration.[6] Congress sought to limit the number of visas allocated to such persons by restricting the family categories in the immigration system. This effort was

---

1 *See, e.g., id.* at 100.

2 *Id.*

3 *See, e.g.,* Johnson, *OPENING THE FLOODGATES, supra* note 18, at 235 ("In operation, the diversity visa programs makes the immigration stream whiter than it would be were the system not in place.").

4 *See, e.g.,* Hing, *supra* note 23, at 101.

5 Immigration Act of 1990, 8 U.S.C § 1153 (1990).

6 *See, e.g.,* Hing, *supra* note 23, at 109, 111.

spearheaded by one of the leading anti-immigration proponents in the history of the United States Senate, Senator Alan Simpson of Wyoming. Simpson had a long history in the Senate of introducing anti-immigrant legislation and continually typified and represented the white supremacist mentality of anti-immigrant forces within the country.[1]

The assault on persons of color intensified with the inauguration of the 42nd President of the United States, Bill Clinton. Soon after Clinton took office, he began to increase border control efforts to reduce illegal immigration from Mexico.[2] These efforts backfired and actually led to "more rather than less Mexican population growth in the United States,"[3] as illegal immigrants crossed unpatrolled areas where they were less likely to be caught, and then were much less likely to return to Mexico once they made it to the U.S.[4] The other major effect of Clinton's efforts was "a tripling of the death rate at the border."[5] This increased death rate was not merely a regrettable side effect, but was in fact entirely foreseeable, and some even claim that the government's "policy was deliberately formulated to maximize the physical risks of Mexican migrant workers, thereby ensuring that hundreds of them would die."[6]

On September 30, 1996, the Illegal Reform and Immigrant Responsibility Act was signed into law, with the strong backing of the Clinton administration: "Enacted in the shadow of the Oklahoma City bombing, and with the support of the Clinton administration and a Republican Congress, the Act was labeled the Illegal Immigration Reform Act. . . . However, the term 'illegal' was a misnomer

---

1 *See, e.g., id.* (noting that Simpson had engaged in efforts "to reduce the Asian- and Latino- dominated family categories" and was interested in programs that "could attract *real* American stock — those who were not Asian or Latino").

2 Douglas S. Massey, *Backfire at the Border: Why Enforcement Without Legalization Cannot Stop Illegal Immigration*, CATO INSTITUTE'S CENTER FOR TRADE POLICY STUDIES, June 13, 2005, at 4, *available at* http://www.freetrade.org/pubs/pas/tpa-029.pdf.

3 *Id.* at 12.

4 *Id.* at 1.

5 *Id.*

6 Johnson, *OPENING THE FLOODGATES, supra* note 18, at 112 (citing Jorge A. Vargas, *U.S. Border Patrol Abuses, Undocumented Mexican Workers, and International Human Rights*, 2 SAN DIEGO INT'L LJ. 1, 69 (2001)).

because the main thrust of the law was all about restricting legal immigration, not only about controlling [illegal immigration]."[1]

The 1996 Act for all intents and purposes gutted the law of political asylum.[2] First, it changed the law so that applicants were required to file their applications for asylum within one year of entry into the United States or forever lose their right to apply.[3] However, merely getting into the country now became problematic as a result of the provisions of the 1996 Act. That law transferred power from the legal system to immigration officers at U.S. ports of entry (most of whom had little more than high school educations), who now had the power to make on-the-spot adjudications of asylum applicants with no rights of appeal.[4] This power to determine life or death consequences for thousands of would-be asylum applicants was an astonishing development,[5] and yet it received almost no attention.

The effect of the 1996 Act on political asylum was only the opening salvo. The law included attempts by Congress to strip the federal courts of their jurisdiction to hear immigration cases. This "court-stripping" as it commonly known, is not new in the United States, but what was new was the extent to which the government would go to deprive immigrants of fundamental rights of due process.[6]

---

1 Donald S. Dobkin, *The Diminishing Prospects for Legal Immigration: Clinton through Bush*, 19 *ST. THOMAS L. REV.* 329, 331 (2006). Although the law focused primarily on restricting legal immigration, it did include some provisions to tighten border control between the U.S. and Mexico. See Douglas S. Massey, *Backfire at the Border: Why Enforcement Without Legalization Cannot Stop Illegal Immigration*, CATO INSTITUTE'S CENTER FOR TRADE POLICY STUDIES, June 13, 2005, at 4-5, *available at* http://www.freetrade.org/pubs/pas/tpa-029.pdf. Professor Massey notes that the legislation approved funding for the building of additional fences in San Diego and for purchasing new military technology and increasing the number of Border Patrol agents. *Id.* At the same time, the section of the legislation that called for tougher penalties applied to "smugglers, undocumented migrants, and *visitors who entered the country legally* but then overstayed their visas." *Id.* at 5. Again, we see that this legislation went far beyond simply increasing efforts to halt illegal immigrants from entering the country.

2 *Id.* at 332.

3 *Id.* at 329

4 *Id.*

5 Donald S. Dobkin, *Court Stripping and Limitations on Judicial Review of Immigration Cases*, 28 *Justice System J.* 104 (2007).

6 *Id.* at 107.

This Act contained provisions that stripped the federal courts of their jurisdiction to hear immigration cases, which were considered to be "matters of discretion."[1] This included appeals from decisions of immigration officers on everything from immigrant and non-immigrant visas to applications for student visas, visitor visas, and extensions of stay. As the law now stands, only a handful of circuits in the federal court of appeals system recognize the rights of aliens to have their cases heard in federal courts, while the overwhelming majority have sided with the government in depriving immigrants of their constitutional rights.[2]

Because state courts cannot "address the federal government's immigration policies[,] [s]tripping the federal courts of jurisdiction eliminates any judicial check whatsoever."[3] The result is a situation that I have previously described as "tantamount to a de facto elimination of judicial review."[4]

The lack of judicial review is particularly problematic in light of the fact that courts are often the best suited branch of government to address matters of discrimination, such as the racism that underlies much of what occurs in U.S. immigration law. In the famous footnote four of *United States v. Carolene Products Co.*,[5] the Supreme Court recognized that "discrete and insular minorities" present a special situation where the courts cannot simply defer without inquiry to the political process.[6] The Supreme Court has also explicitly stated that "[a]liens as a class are a prime example of a 'discrete and insular' minority for whom such heightened judicial solicitude

---

1 *Id.*

2 *Id.*

3 Lucas Guttentag, *Immigration Reform: A Civil Rights Issue*, 3 *STAN. J. CIV. RTS. & CIV. LIBERTIES* 157, 161 (2007); *see also* Johnson, *OPENING THE FLOODGATES, supra* note 18, at 53 (citing *Chae Chin Ping v. United States (The Chinese Exclusion Case)*, 130 U.S. 581, 606 (1989)) ("The Chinese Exclusion Case, which the Supreme Court has not overruled to this day, held that the political branches of the federal government have the unfettered discretion — denominated "plenary power" — to act in the field of immigration. The Court emphasized unconditionally that Congress's judgment is "conclusive on the judiciary." [The result was a] lack of any judicial check on the excesses of Congress . . . .").

4 Dobkin, *supra* note 106, at 107.

5 304 U.S. § 144 (1938).

6 *Id.* at , 152-53 n.4.

---

is appropriate."[1] Professor Erwin Chemerinsky has noted that courts must apply heightened scrutiny in these situations because "[p]rejudice and the history of discrimination make it less likely that racial and national origin minorities can protect themselves through the political process."[2] In other words, intervention by the courts — meaning judicial review — is most needed when dealing with matters affecting minority groups, such as immigrants. Thus, the lack of judicial review in this area is all the more troublesome.

IV. The Effects of Race and Restrictive Immigration Policy

The current restrictive U.S. immigration policy — a policy that has been shaped, and continues to be shaped, by race[3] — has numerous detrimental effects. Aside from the obvious effects on immigrants, potential immigrants, and their family members, immigration restraints have also negatively impacted many others and could have devastating effects on the American economy.

Numerous commentators have noted that the American economy has suffered greatly from the current restrictive environment. As mentioned earlier, restrictive policies have led to foreign investment from countries such as Hong Kong entering Canadian and other markets, rather than supporting U.S. economic interests. [4]

Tourism provides an even clearer example. A recent interview with Jonathan Tisch, the chairman of the Travel Business Roundtable, noted that U.S. immigration is the "worst in the world" and has led to a sharp decline in tourism:

Tisch . . . believes that potential visitors consider trips to the America to be "problematic." This is making the U.S. culturally isolated and is also having a knock-on effect on the economy. "Travel is the number one industry in the world (according to World Travel

---

1 *Graham v. Richardson*, 403 U.S. 365, 372 (1971).

2 Erwin Chemerinsky, *CONSTITUTIONAL LAW: PRINCIPLES AND POLICIES* 669 (Aspen Publishers 2d ed. 2002).

3 *See supra* Parts II-III.

4 *See supra* note 88 and accompanying text.

& Tourism Council figures), but the U.S. is not benefitting," he said.[1]

Tisch has called for "a fresh approach to tourism" that would involve "fewer visa restrictions."[2]

Another big worry about restrictive immigration policies is that these policies interfere with American businesses that depend upon a steady influx of foreign talent. The "undereducation of Americans" has at various times led to efforts by American businesses to relax immigration requirements so that they can bring in "highly skilled immigrants to satisfy a growing vacuum in the labor pool."[3] In the instances where business interests succeeded in their lobbying efforts to convince Congress to allow more skilled immigrants to enter the country, it was usually done in a way that excluded persons of color: "Whatever reform came about, it was always with an eye toward what color or ethnic background qualified immigrants would bring, rather than simply what skills they could offer."[4] Still, in the past, Congress (whatever its motives may have been) was at least willing to entertain the possibility of facilitating an influx of foreign talent, whereas now the business community cannot hope for any such measures, and foreign scientists and engineers are increasingly choosing to work in other countries. Professor Richard Florida has noted that in the post-September 11 climate, visa and green card restrictions, combined with an isolationist foreign policy, has led to a sharp decline in the amount of foreign talent entering the country: "In effect, for the first time in our history, we're saying to highly mobile and very finicky global talent, 'You don't belong here.'"[5]

This restrictive environment has led to massive drops in the number of foreign students applying to study in the U.S., as well as declines in the number of visiting scholars and foreign researchers.[6] Difficulties in getting visas for foreign scientists has led to decisions to host major scientific conferences in other countries, and "for the first time in modern memory — perhaps in the history of our coun-

---

1 Tom Chesshyre, U.S. *Immigration "Worst in the World,"* TIMES ONLINE, Oct. 25, 2007, http://travel.timesonline.co.uk/tol/life_and_style/travel/news/article2739096
2 *Id.*
3 Hing, *supra* note 23, at 108.
4 *Id.* At 111
5 Richard Florida, THE FLIGHT OF THE CREATIVE CLASS 115 (Harper Collins 2005).
6 *Id.* At 111.

try — top scientists and intellectuals from elsewhere are choosing not to come here."[1]

Restrictive immigration policies have even more direct financial consequences on the American economy: "Visa delays alone have cost U.S. businesses roughly $30 billion in two years, according to a June 2004 study . . . ."[2] Major companies such as Exxon Mobil have decided to set up conference offices in London to meet with foreign nationals because U.S. visas have become too hard to obtain. In all of these ways, current U.S. immigration policy has become a major impediment to future progress.

Conclusion

U.S. immigration policy has been — and continues to embrace — racial considerations. The U.S. has rejected color-based discrimination in many other areas, and yet vestiges of historical racism continue to prevail in modern immigration policy. This state of affairs is all the more worrisome given that these same policies have numerous negative effects on the country as a whole. In this sense, the American economy cannot afford to continue the restrictive immigration policies that are now in place.

The U.S. needs to change its current immigration policy to work toward eliminating the vestiges of ant-immigrant racism that currently prevails. This means, at the very least, relaxing visa and green card requirements, as well as streamlining these processes to eliminate long delays. Some scholars advocate going much further and adopting a general "open borders" approach to immigration.[3] Whatever approach the U.S. decides to take, it must be done in a way that is sensitive to the lasting effects of color-based discrimination. Racism has permeated U.S. immigration policy for centuries, and it will likely take a long time to undo all that has been done. To succeed in this endeavor, the U.S. will need help from all branches of government, including the courts, which will need to find ways to reinstate judicial review over important immigration matters. Only then can we hope for a more reasonable approach to U.S. immigration policy.

---

1 *Id.* at 121
2 Id.
3 *See, e.g.,* Kevin R. Johnson, *Open Borders?*, 51 *UCLA L. Rev.* 193 (2003).

9. Why No One Wants Immigration Reform

In a country blessed with so many brilliant and talented individuals, it is truly startling that it is so difficult to reform our deeply flawed immigration system.

Why is this so one might ask? To be sure, this is not an easy question to answer. A good starting point, however, would be to highlight the sobering fact that the last major presidential candidate to actively support comprehensive reform with an immigration amnesty lost the election.

That presidential candidate, Senator John McCain, was one of the original sponsors of the Comprehensive Immigration Reform Act, yet by 2007 had become a staunch opponent of amnesty as he realized his pro-immigration stance was a death knell within the Republican Party, and likely with a large part of the electorate. President Obama, while he gave lip service to comprehensive immigration reform, actually spent little political capital trying to push it through a gridlocked Congress during his first term, and instead used administrative means to implement a limited version of the DREAM Act for long-term undocumented immigrants who entered as children. Simply put, immigration is a hot tamale, and anyone who gets it wrong, proceeds at their own peril.

Traditionally, Democrats have been viewed as more pro-immigration than Republicans. But, in fact, both parties support immigration, but of two different types. Democrats have favored family-based immigration over employment-based immigration, in part because of traditional objections of trade unions but in reality because of the strong ethnic constituencies supporting Democrats in many areas of the United States. Republicans have historically favored expanding employment-based immigration, because a large part of their base owns hotels, restaurants, and other service businesses and agriculture that need a ready supply of labor. That, however, is where the over-simplification ends.

The last nationwide immigration amnesty was in 1986 under Republican President Ronald Reagan. The table below provides a brief overview of the major immigration reform legislation that has passed in the last 30 years:

Year	Name of Bill	Brief Summary of Some of the Major Provisions
1986	Immigration Reform and Control Act of 1986 (Simpson-Mazzoli Act)	• provided amnesty to around 3 million immigrants—namely, certain seasonal agricultural immigrants and immigrants who entered the U.S. before January 1, 1982, and had resided there continuously since then • to obtain amnesty, these immigrants had to admit guilt and pay a fine and any back taxes that were due • employers were now required to attest to their employees' immigration status, and it was made a crime to knowingly hire or recruit undocumented immigrants

1990	Immigration Act of 1990	• increased limits on legal immigration from 500,000 new immigrants per year to 700,000 per year • created the "diversity" visa program • increased annual limits on permanent-job related visas and temporary work visas, and set up priority programs (EB-1 through EB-5) for certain immigrants such as professionals, those with advanced degrees, and those who invest in job-creating ventures • allowed for the granting of temporary protected status to immigrants from countries where it would not be safe for them to return home
1996	Illegal Immigration Reform and Immigrant Responsibility Act of 1996	• increased border security through measures such as hiring more border control agents and building more border fences • barred immigrants from applying for legal status for years if unlawfully present for more than 180 days • gave INS officers broad authority to bar entry to and deport immigrants without any judicial review
2005	REAL ID Act of 2005	• created federal standards for driver's licenses and other forms of ID, making it more difficult for immigrants to obtain such documentation • allowed federal government to grant itself a waiver from laws impeding the building of border fences • allowed deportation for terrorist activity, including membership in designated terrorist organizations • made it more difficult to obtain political asylum
2006	Secure Fence Act of 2006	• increased border security through measures such as authorizing the building of 700 miles of border fences between the U.S. and Mexico

In addition, there have been many other major proposals for immigration reform that have failed to pass. The most famous of these is the 2007 Comprehensive Immigration Reform Act, but other failed legislation includes bills such as the DREAM Act (Development, Relief, and Education for Alien Minors), which was introduced in 2001, 2009, 2010, and 2011, but failed to obtain legislative approval from both chambers.

In 1986, when the Simpson-Mazzoli Act was passed, the country was "booming," at least in comparison to today's anemic economy. Around 3 million immigrants were "legalized." There was broad bipartisan support for the legislation.

The current political landscape is quite different than under the Reagan-Bush White House and the Tip O'Neill Congress. The Tea Party Wing of the Republicans today is generally seen as a solid obstructionist wall blocking immigration reform. Led by a hardline restrictionist right wing of the party, they are diametrically opposed to any amnesty deal or any form of immigrant legalization. They employ law-and-order rhetoric to opine that illegal immigrants are criminals and should not be rewarded for their illegality by being handed the precious "greencard." Nor should illegals be entitled to "jump to the front of the line" over those who have chosen to apply legally for immigration and have waited years. They are consumed with the issue of border enforcement and take the position that until we "seal up" our borders, we shouldn't even consider reforming the system. Democrats on the other hand "talk" immigration reform, but the reality is that during the first two years of President Obama's initial term as President, when the Democrats controlled Congress, he was consumed with passage of Obamacare, and did not seem overly concerned with immigration reform for the remainder of his first term.

During 2009 and 2010, when Democrats controlled both chambers of Congress, but Republicans retained the ability to filibuster unwanted legislation, President Obama made very little attempt to persuade the couple of Republican Senators he needed to pass a bill to support immigration reform. It was only in the last days of his first term that President Obama executed an Executive Order staying the deportation of thousands of DREAM Act students who found themselves illegally in the US through "no fault of their own." No doubt, politics and the attempt to solicit the support of the Hispanic community were central to that decision. Indeed, given how crucial the Hispanic vote was to Obama's reelection, this was arguably the most savvy political move Obama made in the lead-up to the 2012 election, where he garnered over 70 percent of the Hispanic vote, nationwide and in several key battleground states.[1]

Then there are the individual interest groups and major players in the immigration landscape. Each of these groups supports immigration reform of one kind or another. Sometimes their interests align, and sometimes they are diametrically opposed. Certain issues, such as tighter border security, have broader-based support, while other issues create sharp dividing lines, particularly with regard to the most controversial issue of granting amnesty to undocumented immigrants living in the U.S.

On one side of the debate, there are pro-immigration groups that embrace increasing legal immigration of all kinds and granting amnesty to undocumented workers. A number of groups connected to the Hispanic community fall into this category. For instance, the National Council of La Raza, the nation's largest national Hispanic civil rights and advocacy group, has long supported comprehensive immigration reform. Same for the League of United Latin American Citizens (LULAC). And although Hispanic groups have historically been the most vocal supporters of comprehensive immigration reform, other minority groups have pushed for reform efforts as well. For instance, the Asian American Justice Center has noted that around 10 percent of Asian Americans are undocumented, and has joined hands with other groups in support of comprehensive immigration reform, noting that "bring[ing] undocumented families out of the shadows" is one of their "top issues."[2]

Another group that supports immigration reform is the National Immigration Forum, which has spent the last 30 years pro-

---

1 *President Exit Polls, Election 2012*, N.Y. TIMES, http://elections.nytimes.com/2012/results/president/exit-polls.

2 Michelle J. Nealy, *National Immigration Forum Launches New Immigration Reform Campaign*, June 4, 2009, *available at* http://diverseeducation.com/article/12616/.

moting pro-immigration national policies, including reform efforts to increase legal immigration and to grant amnesty (which they refer to as a "pathway to citizenship") to those immigrants who are already here. Also, while many other pro-immigration groups have remained silent on the issue of border control, or have aligned themselves with anti-immigration groups calling for stricter border controls such as increased fencing and patrolling, the National Immigration Forum has not shied away from speaking out in favor of a more "fiscally responsible and humane" approach to border control.[1]

The American Immigration Lawyers Association has also pushed for a comprehensive immigration reform bill.[2] This group, which has 11,000 members with expertise in all aspects of immigration law and policy, supports increasing legal immigration both to reunite families (as Democrats have traditionally supported) and to provide our employers in the STEM fields with more qualified employees (as Republicans have traditionally supported).[3] As for undocumented workers who currently live in the U.S., the American Immigration Lawyers Association explicitly disavows "amnesty"—knowing that this word is the bogey-man of the anti-immigration crowd—but then goes on to voice strong support for what it refers to as "earned legalization."[4] In other words, undocumented workers should be granted amnesty, but only after they "undergo a rigorous process" and pay "substantial penalties."[5]

The immigration reform effort has many other allies that represent a diverse group of interests. For instance, some environmental groups have weighed in on immigration policy. Concerns over the environmental impacts of border walls, which can fragment populations of endangered species, has led the Sierra Club, the Defenders of Wildlife, and the Center for Biological Diversity to support an immigration policy that ensures the protection of "wildlife, com-

---

1 *About the National Immigration Forum*, http://immigrationforum.org/about.

2 *A Resource Guide on Immigration, available at* http://www.aila.org/content/default.aspx?docid=38920.

3 *Ibid.* 4-5.

4 *Ibid.* 12-13.

5 *Ibid.*

munities, and natural resources from damage wrought by border walls between the U.S. and Mexico."[1]

And while most organized labor groups have historically opposed immigration reform, out of the (unfounded) fear that any increase in immigration would decrease the amount of jobs available to native-born workers, the Service Employees International Union has been a long-time supporter of immigration reform. This labor union, which has over two million members, around 25% of which are immigrants, endorses comprehensive immigration reform that includes an amnesty component to ensure a "realistic and expeditious mechanism" for undocumented workers to obtain citizenship.[2]

Comprehensive immigration reform also has substantial support from the business community. While traditional hard-line conservative groups like The Heritage Foundation and Talk Radio have consistently opposed any immigration reform that includes amnesty or another pathway to citizenship for undocumented workers, immigration reform has found support in what may seem like unlikely places. For instance, an immigration policy analyst for the libertarian Cato Institute recently spoke about the need to simultaneously grant amnesty to undocumented workers and pass immigration reform that includes "increasing legal immigration, and not just for highly skilled workers."[3] That same analyst also discussed the views of another conservative commentator who supports promising "amnesty right up front."[4]

Another group that supports comprehensive immigration reform for business reasons is ImmigrationWorks USA, which organizes business owners to support reform efforts. This group advocates increasing worker visas so that U.S. employers have access to

1 Press Release, *Comprehensive Immigration Reform Bill Gets it Right at the Border* (December 15, 2009), http://action.sierraclub.org/site/MessageViewer?em_id=149041.0&dlv_id=129101.

2 *SEIU Principles for Comprehensive Immigration Reform*, http://www.seiu.org/a/immigration/seiu-principles-for-comprehensive-immigration-reform.php.

3 Alex Nowrasteh, *Immigration Reform Should Boost All Skill Levels*, POLITICO, December 13, 2012, *available at* http://www.cato.org/publications/commentary/immigration-reform-should-boost-all-skill-levels.

4 *Ibid.*

the labor force they need. It engages in educational and grassroots efforts to pressure Congress into passing comprehensive immigration reform. As one example, ImmigrationWorks USA has worked with farm and restaurant owners to make sure that they tell their congressional representatives about the need for comprehensive immigration reform.[1]

The tech sector, led by Bill Gates, has also supported immigration reform, making a perennial call for additional H-1B numbers, and more quietly struggling to try to reform USCIS's restrictive policies on L-1B Specialized Knowledge Workers, but to no real avail. There's been little effort to coordinate business with the Hispanic community and other allies needed to push through a coalition comprehensive immigration reform effort. The result has been no amnesty, no reform. Hispanic groups appear to want amnesty or nothing. The tech sector is seemingly only concerned with its own need for highly skilled workers and a way to cut mounting compliance costs and enforcement risks. But the big picture comprehensive immigration reform approach is hard to put together in such a lousy economy plagued by high unemployment.

Even if all of the pro-immigration groups were better organized and could band together to push for reform, they would have to contend against a large number of anti-immigration organizations such as the Federation for American Immigration Reform (FAIR) and NumbersUSA. These groups, along with others like them, actively push for caps and cuts in immigration. FAIR and NumbersUSA work with Talk Radio and internet groups to effectively block any reform legislation by drumming up nativist fears and conspiracy theories with a stock cast of Mexican gunrunners, illegal immigrants bankrupting the nation's welfare programs, and human waves of Indian computer programmers clamoring ashore to take "American jobs." For instance, when the Comprehensive Immigration Reform Act of 2007 was proposed, the website of a group called The American Voice Institute of Public Policy encouraged people

---

1 Stephen Dinan, *Pro-immigration groups ready to fight*, WASHINGTON TIMES, January 11, 2010.

to contact Senators and voice their opposition to the bill that this group claimed would "plunge America into a third world nation."[1]

These groups are not shy about touting the impact they have had on national immigration policy. For instance, NumbersUSA claims on its website that the Comprehensive Immigration Reform Act of 2007 "failed mostly because to the efforts of NumbersUSA's activists faxing and phone call campaigns to the senators' offices."[2] As the *New York Times* noted in an editorial at the end of May 2007, proponents of comprehensive immigration reform found themselves "overmatched by the ferocity of the opposition from the restrictionist right, with talk radio lighting up over 'amnesty,' callers spitting out the words with all the hate they can pour into it."[3]

Other groups like The Heritage Foundation, a conservative think tank, have actively opposed comprehensive immigration reform. The Heritage Foundation was quick to characterize the Comprehensive Immigration Reform Act of 2007 as "the amnesty bill," and later issued a statement celebrating the defeat of that bill: "In rejecting amnesty for illegal immigrants, today's Senate vote was a victory for those who believe in the rule of law."[4] Similar statements were made by some of the Republican Senators who led the charge to defeat the Comprehensive Immigration Reform Act of 2007, including Jim DeMint, who claimed that "the American people won today" by refusing to pass immigration reform.[5] Interestingly, Jim DeMint—often described as an "immigration hawk—recently left the Senate to become President of The Heritage Foundation, ensuring that this conservative think tank will continue to oppose any effort at comprehensive immigration reform.

---

1 The American Voice Institute of Public Policy, *Capital Hill Watch Alert*, http://www. americanvoiceinstitute.org/Comprehensive%20Immigration%20Reform%20 Act%20of%202007%20%20Action%20Alert.htm.

2 NumbersUSA, *Amnesty*, https://www.numbersusa.com/content/issues/amnesty. html.

3 *Editorial*, N.Y. TIMES, May 29, 2007.

4 Ed Fuelner, *Feulner on the Senate Amnesty Bill*, June 27, 2007, http://www.heritage.org/ research/reports/2007/06/feulner-on-the-senate-amnesty-bill.

5 Robert Pear & Carl Huse, *Immigration Bill Fails to Survive Senate Vote*, N.Y. TIMES, June 28, 2007, http://www.nytimes.com/2007/06/28/washington/28cnd-immig. html?_r=0.

The role of Talk Radio on the immigration debate also cannot be underestimated. One Senator who opposed the Comprehensive Immigration Reform Act of 2007 stated that Talk Radio was "a big factor" in the defeat of that law.[1] A study that was released shortly after the defeat of the Comprehensive Immigration Reform Act of 2007 confirmed that Talk Radio helped ensure the bill's demise by convincing people that the proposed legislation was primarily an amnesty bill.[2]

The Comprehensive Immigration Reform Act of 2007

Just a few months after becoming the 43rd President of the United States, George W. Bush went to Ellis Island and announced that immigration reform was a major priority of his new administration:

Immigration is not a problem to be solved. It is a sign of a confident and successful nation. And people who seek to make America their home should not be met in that spirit by representatives of our government. New arrivals should be greeted not with suspicion and resentment, but with openness and courtesy. As many immigrants can testify, that standard has not always been observed. For those seeking entry, the process is often a prolonged ordeal full of complexities and burdens. I'm committed to changing this with INS reforms that treat every immigrant with respect and fairness.[3]

The closest we came to comprehensive immigration reform in recent decades was in 2007 under President Bush, a staunch supporter of the legislation. Originally crafted and introduced as bipartisan legislation from Senators McCain and Kennedy, it took years for the 761-page bill to reach a vote in 2007. In April 2007, most pundits and President Bush expressed optimism about the bill's chances for passage. The next month, when the bill was formally introduced, it became clear that there would be speed bumps, but the bill still seemed to be on track.

All was going well, or so it seemed, until five last-minute amendments were introduced mostly by Republicans but some by Demo-

---

1 *Ibid.*

2 Mike Allen, *Talk radio helped sink immigration reform*, POLITICO, August 20, 2007, *available at* http://www.politico.com/news/stories/0807/5449.html.

3 Remarks by the President at an INS Naturalization Ceremony, July 7, 2001

crats. Two of these so-called "bill-killing" amendments would have weakened the "guest worker" provisions of the bill, by sunsetting the program after five years. Two of the other so-called "bill-killing" amendments provided for granting temporary work status to immigrants waiting for amnesty. The other would have made it easier for such people to get work by requiring that they leave the U.S. first. Texas Senator Kay Bailey Hutchinson opposed the bill which provided a path to legalization for undocumented immigrants. It would have required family members to exit the U.S., return to their native countries and apply at a U.S. Embassy abroad for the immigrant visa. There was general agreement on this provision until at the last moment Hutchinson introduced an amendment requiring that head of households also exit the country and return home, in addition to remaining family members. While this amendment was eventually defeated, this along with other bill-killing amendments crafted largely by Republicans, effectively ended any chance of passage.

In the end, although the bill had been carefully crafted to appeal to both parties, around a third of Senate Democrats joined over three-fourths of Senate Republicans to kill the bill.[1] With 53 Senators against moving on to a final vote and only 46 in favor, supporters fell dramatically short of the 60 votes needed to overcome the delaying tactics (cloture) and parliamentary maneuvers that had dogged the bill for weeks.[2] With no way to cut off debate, Senate Majority Leader Harry M. Reid (D-Nev.) pulled the bill from the Senate floor for a second time.[3]

The rancor that was evident in the defeat of the 2007 bill is understandable given the fact that most Americans opposed immigration reform by almost 70 percent. Senator Jeff Sessions (R-Ala) described the bill's failure as "a crushing defeat, [e]xceeding my expectations."[4] Senate Majority Leader Harry Reid (D-Nev)

1 http://www.govtrack.us/congress/votes/110-2007/s235.
2 *Ibid.*
3 Nicole Gaouette, Senate buries immigration bill, LOS ANGELES TIMES, June 29, 2007.
4 Jeff Sessions, *A Crushing Defeat for the Immigration Bill*, THE HILL, June 28, 2007, http://thehill.com/blogs/congress-blog/politics/

declared, "the big winner today was obstruction."[1] Mexican President Felipe Calderon said the Senate had made a "great mistake" in rejecting the bill. "The U.S. economy cannot keep going without migrant labor," he said.[2]

Did Senator Obama Kill the McCain Immigration Reform Bill?

Barack Obama, then Senator Obama, had long been on record as a supporter of comprehensive immigration reform. Much, however, has been written about Obama's last-minute support of the five "killer" amendments that were largely seen as the unraveling of the immigration bill. So what actually happened?

Obama voted for the five "killer" amendments. Two of those amendments would have weakened the "guest worker" provisions of the bill, by sunsetting the program after five years and lowering the annual quota for the first five years. Two of the other amendments Obama voted for would have made it easier for amnesty applicants to gain temporary worker authorization during the process. The other amendment would have made it easier for such people to get work visas by eliminating the requirement that they had to leave the U.S. first.[3]

The theory that Obama was responsible for the death of the Comprehensive Immigration Reform Act of 2007 rests on the fact that he provided the tie-breaking vote in favor of the amendment to require the "guest worker" provisions to sunset altogether after five years. According to some, this 49-48 vote "was essentially a deal breaker for most Republicans": "[o]nce the guest worker provision had been set to sunset most Republicans were unwilling to support the bill with a yes vote."[4] One thing that this amendment did was cement the view that the bill was no longer bipartisan—a view that was also fueled by reports that the passage of this amendment was driven by the lobbying efforts of organized labor, which was play-

---

1 Gaouette, *Ibid.*

2 *Ibid.*

3 Roger Algase, *ILW blog*, May 25, 2011.

4 Jessica Bastian, *Strange Bedfellows: The Road to Comprehensive Immigration Policy in 2007*, CRITIQUE: A WORLDWIDE JOURNAL OF POLITICS, at 174, *available at* http://lilt.ilstu.edu/critique/Spring2010%20docs/Bastian_Jessica.pdf.

ing a much bigger role in 2007 than it did the year before. It was well known that organized labor was intent on altering the "guest worker" provisions so that employers would have to pay higher wages, thereby making those jobs more attractive to native-born Americans.[1]

One problem with this argument is that the "guest worker" program was never all that popular to begin with. Indeed, it was one of the reasons that some long-time proponents of immigration reform had opposed this bill right from the start. For instance, just after the Senate introduced the bill, LULAC voted unanimously to oppose the bill.[2] LULAC noted that the "guest worker" program "alone would create a new underclass of easily exploited workers who would be forbidden from realizing the American Dream."[3] And many opponents of immigration reform also opposed the "guest worker" program because they considered it to be a pseudo-amnesty. Thus, the decision to sunset an already unpopular "guest worker" program cannot have been what killed immigration reform.

Nevertheless, Republicans accused Obama of "stabbing them in the back" by voting for the "killer" amendments after having been "taken in" to the McCain inner sanctum of immigration reform. Democrats deny this, saying that Obama believed that the amendments would help gain passage of the bill and that McCain, although he still supported the bill, had waned in his enthusiasm for the immigration bill as he saw that his strong support was detrimental to his Presidential election chances because it would be used against him in the Republican primary.

So what really was the most plausible reason the bill failed? My conclusion is that amnesty killed the bill. A significant core of hard-line Republicans opposed even the thought of amnesty, and middle-of-the-road Republicans failed to win over their hard-line colleagues. One commentator even described the watershed event

---

1 *Ibid.* 165-166.
2 LULAC Press Release, May 21, 2007, *available at* http://www.lulac-wisconsin.org/images/LULAC_Opposes_Senate_Immigration_Compromise_In_Current_Form.pdf.
3 *Ibid.*

that killed the bill as "opposition to amnesty—an avalanche of right wing anti-Mexican racism."[1]

Major immigration reform is incredibly difficult to achieve. A large core group of the Republican party is opposed to amnesty. And because of politics one can understand their reluctance to support amnesty. After all, with approximately 70% of the Hispanic vote going for the Democrats, why would the Republicans be interested in legalizing 12 million undocumented immigrants, most of whom will wind up voting for Democrats? Republicans would, in effect, be voting themselves out of office permanently!

Indeed, that is precisely the argument that was put forward by Rush Limbaugh in his staunch opposition to the Comprehensive Immigration Reform Act of 2007, which he referred to as the "Destroy the Republican Party Act."[2] According to Limbaugh, immigration reform was nothing more than a thinly veiled attempt by Democrats to create "a brand-new electorate" of the voting-age portion of the 12 million undocumented immigrants to help Democrats "win election after election after election."[3]

The only immigration policy that practically all Republicans have consistently supported is increased border protections. Indeed, another explanation for why the 2007 immigration reform bill failed is that the delicate coalition of supporters for comprehensive immigration reform began to fall apart a year earlier when Congress passed the Secure Fence Act of 2006. This Republican-driven bill, which called for building 700 miles of new fencing at the U.S.-Mexico border, passed with overwhelming support in both chambers. Roughly a third of the Democrats in the House and Senate voted in favor of this bill, and over 97% of Republicans in both chambers supported the bill.[4]

President Bush signed the Secure Fence Act of 2006 out of "party loyalty," even though he had been actively lobbying Republican Senators and Representatives to pass comprehensive immigration

---

1 Algase, *Ibid.*
2 Peter Wallsten, *Wall divides Republican Party factions*, L.A. TIMES, June 3, 2007,
3 *Ibid.*
4 http://www.govtrack.us/congress/votes/109-2006/h446 (House vote) & http://www.govtrack.us/congress/votes/109-2006/s262 (Senate vote).

reform, rather than piecemeal bills like this one.[1] President Bush knew that a piecemeal approach to immigration reform was problematic because border protection was the only immigration concern for a number of hard-line Republicans, who viewed undocumented immigrants as a threat to national security and were not interested in hearing about the benefits of immigration. Of course, some of those hard-liners were probably never going to support comprehensive immigration reform anyways, but some of them may have been willing to back such a proposal if it were the only way to achieve increased border security. But once they got the bill they wanted, they no longer had any interest in taking part in comprehensive immigration reform.

And the Secure Fence Act of 2006 also pulled the rug out from more moderate Republicans who, like the hard-liners, used national security as a justification for their support for comprehensive immigration reform. Before the Secure Fence Act of 2006, these moderate Republicans could tell their anti-immigration constituents that a bill allowing amnesty was a necessary evil to help ensure greater border security. But once border security went through as a stand-alone measure, comprehensive immigration reform started to look a lot more like simply amnesty, not national security. A pure amnesty bill would garner few, if any, Republican votes, and would have enough defectors from the Democrats to prevent passage. Suddenly the delicate coalition was starting to break apart.

Recognizing that a bill would never pass if it were focused only on amnesty, the Comprehensive Immigration Reform Act of 2007 proposed numerous provisions for beefing up border security beyond what was required by the Secure Fence Act of 2006. Still, the case for an immigration bill to secure our borders became a much harder sell once Congress had already passed a bill that specifically aimed at securing our borders. In short, because a secure borders act had already passed the year before, the Comprehensive Immigration Reform Act of 2007 was generally seen primarily as an amnesty bill.

---

1 Bastian, *Ibid.* 160.

The history of the Comprehensive Immigration Reform Act of 2007 made clear that this is an issue where neither party could count on a united front. Comprehensive immigration reform encompasses so many different—and often conflicting—goals that there is simply no way to bring together all of the divergent views within each party. Indeed, the closest either party has come to a unified front was the Secure Fence Act of 2006, which had virtually universal support among Republicans. But that was only possible because that bill was the polar opposite of *comprehensive* reform— rather than addressing immigration reform at all levels, it singled out one issue (border security) and ignored everything else.

The difficulty of presenting a unified front within each party is why the 2007 effort at comprehensive immigration reform lived and died in the Senate and was never addressed by the House. When Representative Nancy Pelosi took over as Speaker of the House in January 2007, after the Democrats took majority control of that chamber following the 2006 election, she focused all of her efforts on "issues that could easily garner majority support" and deliberately avoided addressing immigration because she "feared splitting and subsequently losing control of her recent majority, understanding that some Democrats would be forced to break from leadership when voting on immigration."[1] Without any help from the House leadership, comprehensive immigration reform was left to the Senate.

The Senate should have been safe ground for the passage of comprehensive immigration reform. After all, the Senate had already passed such a bill the previous session, by a vote of 62 to 36. That bill ended up dying in a conference committee during the summer of 2006, presumably because it contained numerous measures—including an amnesty-like pathway to citizenship—that the House version had rejected. But re-passage in the Senate should have been a cakewalk. After all, the 62 votes for comprehensive immigration reform in 2006 included the support of over 85% of Democratic Senators, and the 2006 election saw the addition of a number of new Democratic Senators as that party took control of the Senate.

---

1 *Ibid.* 162.

Thus, if anything, there should have been *more* votes in favor of comprehensive immigration reform in 2007 than there were in 2006.

But it did not pan out that way. As some commentators have noted, the bill ran into trouble right off the bat:

Since its introduction, various components of the Senate proposal have come under fire from all sides of the debate. Conservative groups said Republican senators who supported the proposal were "caving" on conservative principles of strongly enforcing the border and following the rule of law. Conservatives also opposed the legalization program, which many equated to an amnesty.

On the left, some criticized the merit-based system, claiming it would divide families and mark a drastic change to US immigration policy.

Labor advocates opposed the temporary guest worker program, which they said would create an underclass of workers and bring down the wages of native workers.

Immigrant advocacy groups said that the application fee for the Z visa, which could cost up to $9,000 for a family of four, was too high and the "touchback" provision too burdensome. Further, they said the bill placed too many overall restrictions on immigrants seeking a path to legalization/citizenship.

Employers were also unhappy with the legislation, claiming it would not cure the severe labor shortages they foresee in the coming decade. Employers of high-skilled workers said the merit-based points system would "take the hiring decision out of [employers'] hands and place it in the hands of the federal government." Employers of low-skilled workers claimed that a merit-based system would be skewed in favor of more highly skilled and educated workers, resulting in labor shortages in certain industries.[1]

In short, in attempting to put together a coalition of supporters, the proponents of the Comprehensive Immigration Reform Act of 2007 ended up simultaneously creating a coalition of opponents who, while perhaps supportive of some provisions of the bill, were unwilling to tolerate those provisions that they disfavored.

---

1 Policy Beat, June 15, 2007, http://www.migrationinformation.org/USfocus/display. cfm?id=607.

The bill eventually failed by a vote of 46 to 53 to obtain the cloture vote that was needed for passage. How did Comprehensive Immigration Reform go from having 62 votes in the Senate in 2006 to just 46 votes one year later? The answer is that Republican support for the bill dropped precipitously. While the 2006 bill had the support of 22 Republicans, a year later there were only 11 Republicans who voted in favor of cloture on the 2007 bill.[1] This sharp decline can only be explained by a ramping up of the anti-amnesty rhetoric among hard-line Republicans, who were able to bring more moderate Republicans into their camp after passage of the Secure Fence Act of 2006. Once the issue of border security had been cleaved off, the bill started to look less like a bipartisan effort and more like a bill that was being driven only by Democrats.

The amnesty provisions of the Comprehensive Immigration Reform Act of 2007 led some prominent hard-line Republican Senators to deem the bill "dead on arrival" before it was even formally introduced.[2] Although the bill never made it through the Senate, even if it had, a number of hard-line Republican House members were on record taking a similar stance and noting that there was "overwhelming opposition in the U.S. House to the Senate immigration bill."[3]

In the end, it was not Obama that killed the Comprehensive Immigration Reform Act of 2007. It was amnesty.

Current Efforts at Comprehensive Immigration Reform

The long, tortured history of failed attempts at comprehensive immigration reform took an interesting twist after the 2012 presidential election. The day after President Obama won reelection, the Hispanic community, over 70% of which voted for Obama, took credit for his victory and began making policy demands.[4] The Hispanic vote was suddenly the most important demographic in U.S. electoral politics, and Democrats began shifting even more toward

---

1 http://www.govtrack.us/congress/votes/110-2007/s235.

2 Jerome R. Corsi, *GOP: Immigration Plan "Dead on Arrival,"* WND, May 11, 2007, http://www.wnd.com/2007/05/41544/.

3 Major Garrett, *House Republicans Resolute in Opposition to Senate Immigration Bill,* FOX NEWS, June 26, 2007, http://www.foxnews.com/story/0,2933,286792,00.html.

4 Candace Wheeler, *Advocates hope high Latino voter turnout will lead to immigration policy changes,* WASHINGTON POST, November 8, 2012.

pro-immigration policies, while a number of prominent previously anti-immigration Republicans did an abrupt U-turn and began touting the need for comprehensive immigration reform.

House Speaker John Boehner (R-Oh), for instance, who for years refused to address immigration reform in any way and elevated Republicans with well-known anti-immigration slants into positions of power, surprised many when—just days after the election—he claimed that comprehensive immigration reform is necessary and vowed to work toward achieving it.[1] Other former hard-line anti-immigration Republicans, such as Sean Hannity and Rupert Murdoch, also did an abrupt about-face and began calling for comprehensive immigration reform in the week after the election. Similarly, conservative columnist George Will noted that 2012 is the "year in which election results reinserted immigration into the political conversation" and went on to stake out his position that immigration should be seen as "an entrepreneurial act."[2] In the words of veteran Republican Party strategist Charlie Black, "What you have is agreement that we as a party need to spend a lot of time and effort on the Latino vote."[3] In perhaps the clearest indication that the Republican Party was serious about building bridges with the Hispanic community, former President George W. Bush—who has generally been seen as political kryptonite since he left office four years ago, and was not even invited to speak at this year's Republican National Convention—made a public appearance in early December 2012 to tout the benefits of immigration and the need for immigration reform.[4]

---

1 Elizabeth Llorente, *Speaker John Boehner Changes Hard-line Tone and Pledges Immigration Reform*, FOX NEWS, November 9, 2012, http://latino.foxnews.com/latino/politics/2012/11/09/speaker-john-boehner-changes-hard-line-tone-and-pledges-immigration-reform/.

2 George Will, *America Needs Immigrants as Much as Ever*, WASHINGTON POST, December 26, 2012.

3 *Republican Party Showing Shift on Immigration, Gun Control and Tax Hike*, FOX NEWS LATINO, December 26, 2012, http://latino.foxnews.com/latino/politics/2012/12/26/republican-party-showing-shift-on-immigration-gun-control-and-tax-hike/.

4 Julia Preston, *Praising Immigrants, Bush Leads Conservative Appeal for G.O.P. to Soften Tone*, N.Y. TIMES, December 4, 2012.

The Republican Party's recent outreach to the Hispanic community is simply a matter of political survival. Some commentators have noted that the results of the 2012 election show that the Republican Party faces a "demographic cliff" as it sees ever smaller support each election cycle from a Hispanic population that makes up an ever larger share of the electorate.[1] According to this theory, Republicans "have alienated Latino voters so thoroughly that they risk becoming a regional party unless something big changes, and changes soon."[2] In short, from an electoral-strategy perspective, Republicans' anti-immigration policies have been "a colossal failure."[3] By contrast, President Obama's decision in the summer of 2012 to provide relief from deportation for roughly 1.4 million undocumented workers under age 30 arguably "changed the course of the election" in Obama's favor by increasing enthusiasm for him among Latino and non-Latino supporters of immigrant rights.[4]

The Republican party's current unpopularity among Hispanic voters is viewed as a "demographic cliff" because Hispanic voters have had an increasingly large influence on the last few elections, and will have an even larger impact in the years to come. In a recent study by the Pew Research Center, titled "An Awakened Giant: The Hispanic Electorate Is Likely to Double by 2030," the authors note that the roughly 12 million Hispanics who turned out to vote in 2012 are only a fraction of the 53 million Hispanics that currently reside in the U.S., many of whom (including 17 million Hispanics currently under age 18) will become voters in future elections.[5] The study thus predicts that "generational replacement alone" will change the current number of eligible Hispanic voters from around 23 million "to about 40 million within two decades."[6] Thus, if electoral turnout "over time converges with that of whites and blacks in recent elections (66% and 65%, respectively, in 2008), that would mean twice as many Latino voters could be casting ballots in 2032

1 Lynn Tramonte, *GOP's 'demographic clif' and the new politics of immigration*, December 26, 2012, http://thehill.com/blogs/congress-blog/homeland-security/274551-gops-demographic-cliff-and-the-new-politics-of-immigration.

2 *Ibid.*

3 *Ibid.*

4 *Ibid.*

5 Pew Research Center, *An Awakened Giant: The Hispanic Electorate Is Likely to Double by 2030*, November 14, 2012, *available at* http://www.pewhispanic.org/files/2012/11/hispanic_vote_likely_to_double_by_2030_11-14-12.pdf.

6 *Ibid.*

as did in 2012."[1] And keep in mind that these numbers refer only to Hispanics who are currently U.S. citizens—the doubling of Hispanic voters does not include any of the roughly 12 million undocumented workers (over 7 million of which are already of voting age) who would become eligible for citizenship (and voting rights) if Congress passed comprehensive immigration reform that included an amnesty provision.[2]

Thus, it is not surprising that Republicans are scrambling to find a way to gain traction among this growing demographic. Although some Republicans remain steadfast in their hard-line opposition to immigration reform of any kind, particularly if it includes an amnesty provision, there seems to be a shift occurring among the more moderate members of that party. For instance, a recent article by the conservative pundit and Tea Party gem Ann Coulter led to a harsh backlash from a pro-immigrant faction of the Republican Party, which demanded "an immediate apology for [her] latest anti-Latino and anti-immigrant rant."[3] And pro-immigration groups like the National Immigration Forum are suddenly finding new allies among Republicans, as demonstrated by a December 2012 gathering of traditionally conservative business owners, law enforcement officials, and evangelicals.[4]

While the movement of former hard-line anti-immigrant Republicans has garnered the most media attention in the weeks after the election, it is also noteworthy that Democrats have shifted positions as well, albeit in a more subtle way. President Obama, for instance, is much more outspoken about the need for comprehensive immigration reform, and made a policy statement at the end of November 2012 explicitly calling for amnesty through "establishing a pathway for undocumented individuals to earn their citizenship."[5]

---

1 Ibid.

2 Ibid. 7.

3 Bob Quasius, Sr., *Pro-immigrant GOP Group Slams Ann Coulter for Anti-Latino Bigotry*, TUCSON CITIZEN, December 7, 2012, http://tucsoncitizen.com/arizona-lincoln-republican/2012/12/07/pro-immigrant-gop-group-slams-ann-coulter-for-anti-latino-bigotry/.

4 Stephanie Samuel, *Immigration Coalition Calls Out 'Smal' Anti-Amnesty Faction of GOP*, CP POLITICS, December 5, 2007, http://www.christianpost.com/news/immigration-coalition-calls-out-small-anti-amnesty-faction-of-gop-86073/.

5 Statement of Administration Policy, November 28, 2012, http://www.whitehouse.gov/sites/default/files/omb/legislative/sap/112/saphr6429r_20121128.pdf.

The pressure is mounting, and supporters of comprehensive immigration reform are seizing the moment. A coalition of eight Latino groups informed legislators in early December 2012 that these groups intend to put together scorecards keeping track of each legislator's voting record on immigration reform efforts, and they "promised to widely publicize the scores within the Latino community next time those lawmakers are up for reelection."[1] The coalition noted that it intends to target members of both major parties, and warned that for politicians who fail to support comprehensive immigration reform, the 2014 elections "may not look too pretty."[2]

That said, those skeptical of the prospects of comprehensive immigration reform note that by the end of December 2012, economic issues related to the impending "fiscal cliff" were already pushing immigration reform issues to the back burner.[3] After all, while President George W. Bush was a staunch proponent of comprehensive immigration reform, the sad truth remains that "comprehensive immigration reform was nonexistent under eight years of Bush."[4] Also, there could be a backlash to the zeal with which some Hispanic groups began pushing comprehensive immigration reform in the immediate aftermath of the 2012 election. After all, bipartisanship is needed if a bill is going be embraced by both a Republican-led House and a Democratic-led Senate. Yet, the coalition of eight Latino groups that called for comprehensive immigration reform in early December 2012 did not strike the tone that one would be expect when looking to pass bipartisanship legislation. Not mincing words, one leader of that group told the press that there would be a "massive" grassroots campaign to ensure that Hispanics are informed of (and thus able to vote out of office) anyone who opposes reform efforts: "Comprehensive immigration reform is going to hap-

---

1 Elise Foley, *Immigration Reform's Latino Leaders Warn 2014 'May Not Look Too Pretty' For Opponents*, HUFFINGTON POST, December 12, 2012, http://www.huffington-post.com/2012/12/12/immigration-reform-latino-2014_n_2287598.html.
2 *Ibid.*
3 Michael De Los Santos, *Immigration Reform: Obama Will Struggle With Reform, Despite Strong Latino Support*, POLICYMIC, December 23, 2012, http://www.policymic.com/articles/21348/immigration-reform-obama-will-struggle-with-reform-despite-strong-latino-support.
4 *Ibid.*

pen. Whether it will be over the political bodies of some of the current members of Congress only they can decide."[1]

While a number of Republicans are now making noise about supporting comprehensive immigration reform, it is unclear how deep that support goes. Republicans are in a bit of a quandary when it comes to immigration reform. In short, "Republican leaders who have studied voting statistics are concerned that their party's chances to regain the White House will dwindle if they cannot attract more Latinos."[2] They simply cannot survive future elections if the ever-expanding demographic of Hispanic voters continues to give 70% of its support to Democrats. But the solution to this problem is not clear. If Republicans thought they could flip that number and get Hispanics to vote 70% in favor of Republicans, then they would almost surely support comprehensive immigration reform. But the quandary for Republicans arises from the fact that it is unclear whether a majority of Hispanics will ever support the Republican Party. The best data to date shows that even George W. Bush, who was a staunch proponent of comprehensive immigration reform and received higher approval ratings among Hispanics than any other Republican President, received only around 40% of the Hispanic vote in 2004.[3] Similarly, Ronald Reagan, who believed that "Hispanics are already Republican—they just don't know it yet," hired an advertising guru to help him court Hispanic voters in 1984, but still received only around 40% of the Hispanic vote that year.[4] If at least 6 out of 10 Hispanics are going to vote Democratic even when Republicans reach out to them and take policy positions in support of comprehensive immigration reform, then the most sensible Republican strategy would be to do all they can to prevent legislation that would allow 12 million undocumented immigrants to obtain citizenship and the voting rights that accompany it.

1 Julia Preston, *Latino Groups Warn Congress to Fix Immigration, or Else*, N.Y. TIMES, December 13, 2012, *available at* http://thecaucus.blogs.nytimes.com/2012/12/12/latino-groups-warn-congress-to-fix-immigration-or-else/.

2 *Ibid.*

3 Pew Research Center, *Hispanics and the 2004 Election: Population, Electorate and Voters*, June 27, 2005, at 12, *available at* http://www.pewhispanic.org/files/reports/48.pdf.

4 Ruben Navarrette, Jr., *Remembering Reagan* (2011), http://www.latinomagazine.com/fall2011/journal/reaganremb.htm.

Even better, from a purely strategic standpoint, would be for Republicans to privately oppose immigration reform and use underhanded techniques to keep an amnesty-type bill from passing (thus minimizing the amount of Hispanics eligible to vote), while publicly claiming to support immigration reform (to try to move Hispanic support for Republicans from the less than 30% received by Romney in 2012 to the Bush-era numbers of around 40% in 2004). In December 2012, Republicans, led by Latino Senator Marco Rubio, began hinting at one way they might try to do precisely that—namely, by pushing pro-immigration bills in a piecemeal fashion and addressing immigration issues that have broad-based support "before ever considering granting legal status" to undocumented workers.[1] This approach allows Republicans to appear to be pro-immigration because they are advocating, for instance, an increase in high-tech and other STEM-related visas, while avoiding comprehensive immigration reform that would create a new segment of Democrat-leaning voters. Their hope is that Hispanic voters will view Republicans' support for these piecemeal bills as outweighing the failure to support comprehensive reform efforts that include amnesty.

That may be too fine a line to walk, particularly now that various pro-immigration groups are paying close attention to which legislators support their agenda. But that may be the best option Republicans have if the party seeks to remain viable in future elections. This is particularly true given that President Obama is so wildly popular with Hispanics, and, despite increasing deportations and failing to achieve comprehensive immigration reform in his first four years of office, is generally seen as pro-immigration. By contrast, the Republican Party, led by Mitt Romney's calls for "self-deportation," was seen by the end of the 2012 election as the party that opposes immigration. This means that, going forward, even if Republicans were willing to jump up and down shouting their support for immigration, at the end of the day President Obama and his Democratic Party are likely to gain as much, if not more, credit for the passage of comprehensive immigration reform. That result would be the absolute worst outcome for the Republican Party, which would not only see a rise in the Hispanic voting population, but would also

---

1 Laura Meckler, *Citizenship Becomes Focus of Immigration Fight*, WALL STREET JOURNAL, December 13, 2012.

see Democrats maintaining, or perhaps even increasing, their 70% share of that vote.

Game theorists would describe the situation for Republicans using the following table of possibilities:

Should Republicans Support an Amnesty Bill?	If the Bill Passes and Both Parties Get Credit	If the Bill Passes and Only Democrats Get Credit	If the Bill Fails
	(OPTION 1)	(OPTION 2)	(OPTION 3)
Yes	Republican portion of 12 million current Hispanic voters increases to 40% (netting Republicans 1.2 million votes) 12 million new voters, 7 million immediately eligible to vote→4 million voting, 60% for Democrats (netting Democrats 0.8 million votes) Net effect = 0.4 million additional votes for Republicans (increases as Hispanic turnout increases)	Republicans get 30% of 12 million current Hispanic voters (no net votes to anyone). 12 million new voters, 7 million immediately eligible to vote→4 million voting, 70% for Democrats (netting Democrats 1.6 million votes) Net effect = 1.6 million additional votes for Democrats (increases as Hispanic turnout increases)	Republican portion of 12 million current Hispanic voters increases to 40% (netting Republicans 1.2 million votes) No new Hispanic voters obtaining citizenship through amnesty (no net votes to anyone) Net effect = 1.2 million additional votes for Republicans (increases as Hispanic turnout increases)

		(OPTION 4)	(OPTION 5)
No	X (not possible—if Republicans oppose reform, they will not get credit for it)	Same as above. Net effect = 1.6 million additional votes for Democrats (increases as Hispanic turnout increases)	Republicans get 30% of 12 million current Hispanic voters (no net votes to anyone). Net effect = neither party gains or loses votes

Of course, this is an overly simplistic model. For one thing, it is focused primarily on the immediate elections of 2014 and 2016 and assumes that Hispanic turnout would be similar in those elections as in 2012. But, as noted above, if Hispanic turnout increases sharply, as it is expected to do in the next 20 years, then the winners in the above columns become even greater winners on the whole.[1] Thus, as a long-term strategy, the potential pay-off to Republicans for supporting immigration reform increases immensely if it can somehow end up with Options 1 or 3 (supporting comprehensive immigration reform and either getting joint credit for the bill's passage or seeing the bill fail despite Republican support). With an ever-increasing Hispanic population, if the Republican party can move from receiving 30% support to 40%, that extra 10% would translate to a lot of additional Republican votes, and would more than offset the immediate net loss of around 0.8 million votes from receiving only 40% of the roughly 4 million voters who show up immediately after an amnesty bill is passed. It would even more than offset the greater loss of votes once all 12 million undocumented workers come of voting age, which could make the net vote loss to Republicans from amnesty more like 1.5 million, rather than 0.8 million.

The problem is that not all of the 5 options noted in the table above are equally likely. To the contrary, the best option for Republicans—option 3—is practically impossible. As noted earlier, Republicans seemed to be taking a stab at this outcome in the months after the election when they proposed piecemeal immigration bills that are facially pro-immigration, while at the same time avoiding any amnesty-type provisions. But at some point Democrats are sure to make Republicans take a firm stance on the specific issue of comprehensive immigration reform that includes amnesty. If Republicans come out in favor of comprehensive immigration reform, it is very unlikely that an amnesty provision would fail to pass, given that the vast majority of Democrats and the President support amnesty. The only way that could happen is if Republicans claimed to support the bill, while finding a procedural or technical reason to block its passage (such as claiming that the issue is better dealt with piecemeal). But any scrutiny of such efforts would surely result in Republicans being blamed for the failure to pass comprehensive immigration. In that situation, it is difficult to see how Republicans would gain support among Hispanics voters.

Option 1 is more likely, but even that is probably wishful thinking. As noted in the table above, if comprehensive immigration reform passes, there are three possibilities: option 1, in which Republicans see small, but increasing, gains in votes, or option 2 or 4, which both lead to significantly larger—and increasing—gains for Democrats. And not only are the potential gains to the Democrats larger that the potential gains to the Republicans, but the likelihood of option 1 is pretty minimal relative to the likelihood of option 2 or 4. As noted above, correctly or incorrectly, the 2012 election solidified the view that President Obama and his fellow Democrats are more pro-immigration than Republicans, and Democrats are thus quite likely to take the vast majority of the credit for the passage of comprehensive immigration reform. Consequently, Republicans would be deluding themselves if they thought that the passage of comprehensive immigration reform would result in them receiving increased support from Hispanics in future elections.

If my analysis is correct that Democrats will likely get most of the credit for the passage of comprehensive immigration reform, then option 1, like option 3, is a very unlikely outcome. In football terms, options 1 and 3 might be considered Hail Marys. That leaves options 2, 4, and 5 as the only real options the Republicans have.

And options 2 and 4, which both result in significantly increased voter support for Democrats, are clearly disastrous for the Republican parties' future electoral prospects. Thus, the only real choice that the Republicans have to prevent further losses to Democrats in future elections is option 5, in which they oppose comprehensive immigration reform and succeed in defeating such a bill from passing. From an electoral strategy perspective, that seems to be the best choice of the realistic options facing the Republican Party.

That said, Republicans cannot be happy about maintaining the status quo in which they oppose comprehensive immigration reform and consequently continue to receive only 30% of the Hispanic vote. Given the ever-increasing numbers of Hispanic voters, particularly in a number of key battleground states, this really could mean the end of that party.[1] If the situation really is that desperate, then Hail Marys may be what is needed, and Republicans may end up supporting comprehensive immigration reform in the hope that they will receive credit for it.

Any way you look at it, comprehensive immigration reform depends on a coalition of legislators overcomingjl many obstacles that have prevented such legislation in years past.

1 Tramonte, *Ibid.*

10. Prescriptions to Fix the Mess

At the date of this writing, the national unemployment rate is just shy of 8%, California 9.8%, and Michigan 8.9%. If we include the underemployed, expired unemployment applicants and former workers who have simply given up their job searches, the real un-employment rate is closer to 20%.

In recent years, our economy required a lifesaving infusion of trillions of dollars of stimulus money, money we didn't have, to avert a Depression of cataclysmic proportions. Entire industries have risen and fallen as the roller coaster of our economy twists and turns.

Despite all of these issues and warnings, we continue to deport and turn away immigrants — a solution to many of these challenges — at a record pace. Entrepreneurs, investors and employees of for-eign corporations struggle as never before to obtain visas as U.S. immigration officials raise bureaucratic restrictions. The housing market continues to erode in both price and volume with housing starts nearing all-time lows. Our "recovery" is anemic at best, lack-ing the sparks of demand which ushered in past recoveries.

Self-Evident Announcement

The United States is a combatant in a fierce global competition for people and resources. (Would someone please mention this to the Congress?) These potential U.S. citizens — persons with exceptional brainpower, capital, acumen and manpower — would bring spendable dollars to our economy while also supplying invaluable labor and expertise that drives jobs creation, services, manufacturing, production and more. In the Economics 101 category, these immigrants provide both the supply (labor) and demand (marketplace).

While we allow in just over a million permanent residents a year, Canada admits immigrants at four times our rate per capita, Australia at two times; and both those countries garner the stimulus from those new residents. The housing markets are expanding in those countries and in other fast growing economies, while there are presently not enough people in this country who are qualified to buy up our excess housing inventory.

Medicare, Medicaid and Social Security are seriously underfunded, with fewer young participants entering the system to contribute as the Boomer Generation reaches retirement age. Despite the inflamed rhetoric coming out of Washington, from both sides of the aisle, there are not nearly enough taxpayers who can pay into the system to keep it solvent at present rates. Given the current direction, it is just a matter of time before the system collapses.

Something must be done and *something can be done.* At the core of our problems reside the simple issues: We need to build **demand**, new markets, for our products and services, while also seeking pragmatic solutions to our immigration mess. The solutions are there, but first we need of a complete overhaul of our legal immigration categories and a prescription to cure the problems.

Here, in simple steps, are actions we can and must take to heal ourselves:

1. Create an EB-7 Visa — Invest in a Green Card

An immigrant who purchases a home in excess of $250,000 will be eligible for a green card, subject to clearance, normal background and security checks. Applicants in this category would be investing in the United States in the most fundamental form possible: the purchase of a home. These purchases and the subsequent investments they represent are long term and binding — no one can take that home out of the country.

There are tens of thousands of people around the world who have the means and resources to purchase such homes, and most of them currently reside in countries far below our standard of living. These potential buyers would love to move to the safety, security and relative prosperity of the United States and would become valuable citizens with patriotic passion for our freedoms and opportunities.

This modest, sensible proposal would create a revolution in the real estate, mortgage and financial services industries in this country and kick start a long term foundation to real economic recovery.

Beyond security checks and appropriate immigration documents, applicants would be required to produce statements showing that the real estate purchase transaction had closed and they were now the legal owners. The applicants would be granted a conditional green card for 24 months, similar to immigrant marriages to U.S. citizens. At the end of the 24-month probation period, applicants would provide proof that they continue to own the home and the permanent green card would be issued.

Home sales increase. Home starts reinvigorate. New markets open.

2. Create the Silver Visa — Retire Here

Similar to EB-7 Visa applicants, there are tens of thousands of affluent people around the world who would welcome the opportunity to retire in the U.S. In these cases, the U.S. would grant visas to persons over the age of 55 who would like to retire in the United States and can prove a net worth of $500,000 or more.

In order to avoid burdening Medicare and similar programs, these applicants would be required to purchase and pay for their own medical insurance, regularly demonstrating insurance is updated. Failure to maintain adequate medical coverage would result in the loss of status.

Senior citizens with disposable income — how many states would be competing for these residents?

3. Revamp the Investor and Entrepreneur Visa — Bring Your Money Here

The U.S. currently offers the EB-5 visa, an Investor Visa. Generally speaking, this visa cites an investment of $1,000,000 and a requirement that jobs for 10 U.S. workers be generated.

While the fundamentals are sensible, the criteria for this visa go on and on, sufficiently arcane as to negate its value. The many requirements, onerous to the point of ridiculous, are virtually impossible to meet and a high enough proportion of the investment vehicles and applications fail to gain approval so as to be viewed by prudent potential applicants as an unacceptable risk. This visa category has never attracted enough investors to fill its annual allotment, and in that sense has been a failure.

Some years back, a panel session was convened on Investor Visas at a convention for immigration professionals. As the session was convened, three attorneys entered the room. The moderator saw them and said, "You see those three gentlemen who just came into the room? That's about how many people were approved last year under the investor category!"

In 2003, there were *39 applicants* approved under this category. The number rose to an all-time high of 1,029 in 2008. As barriers to self-employed business owners in other U.S. immigration categories have been raised (we will mention one of these, below, the US-CIS decision known as *NY State Dept. of Transportation* case) the numbers have recently increased to about 5,000 per year. But, any way the numbers are viewed, it is clear that it's time for a radical change.

At the time of this writing, Congress is reviewing a bill titled the EB-6 Visa, which aims to address the gaps and streamline the process inherent in this category. The new bill, sponsored by Senators Lugar and Kerry, would require only a $250,000 investment and a temporary visa would be granted for two years. After that trial period, the Entrepreneur visa would be made permanent if the entrepreneur created at least 5 jobs and attracted $1M in new capital or had revenue of $1M. So far, this initiative has not been passed, and even more work must be done.

We must overhaul the criteria and application process for this visa, to literally capitalize on the billions of investment dollars and untold amount of brainpower, innovation and jobs creating "sweat equity" the U.S. would gain.

4. Expand the Exceptional Student Green Card — Brains Welcome

In 1933, Albert Einstein emigrated to the United States to escape the growing threats of fascism and oppression in Europe. Einstein found a welcoming home at Princeton University, where he continued vital work in quantum mechanics and other subjects. Consider how world history would have been altered had Einstein been barred from the U.S. The fact is, every year future Einsteins are being prohibited from entering the United States.

Every week, stories appear about brilliant foreign students unable to obtain legal status in the U.S. Every year, the U.S. loses out vast resources of brainpower because talented people are forced to find other countries of residence and study.

The U.S. must initiate a pilot program where we identify, say, the top 50 ranked colleges and universities and grant green cards to any graduate of these highly selective institutions. Unlike current practice, we must not limit the visa to graduates to STEM (Science, Technology, Engineering, and Mathematics). Our country needs as many brilliant students and young entrepreneurs as we can attract, not just those in the sciences.

A student who can get accepted to Yale, Stanford, University of Chicago or a Public Ivy and receives a degree from those world-class institutions is a reasonable bet to contribute to the betterment of our country.

The United Kingdom is ahead of us in many applications of this category. In one instance, they have a similar program in place for MBA student/applicants. Graduates of the top 50 MBA schools *in the world* (not just U.K. schools) automatically score enough points to qualify for landed immigrant status in the U.K., the equivalent of our green card. This program has exceeded even the most promising expectations, attracting thousands of high-caliber business minds to London's financial district.

5. Expand the Exceptional or Extraordinary Green Card

As outlined earlier in our book, the U.S. provides categories for extraordinary and exceptional applicants. While the program is promising, the number of approvals required for each applicant demonstrates the need for significant modification.

Lately, there has been some recognition of the unnecessary immigration barriers to entrepreneurial investment, start-ups, and cross-border business formation.

- For the exceptional category, the ridiculous and illegal requirements of NY Dept. of Transportation (NYSDT) were eliminated.1 NYSDT was a decision taken in 1998 by the then Commissioner of Immigration interpreted to bar a National Interest Waiver (NIW) of the labor certification requirement to entrepreneurs. For years, this effectively cut off entrepreneurs from a primary path to a green card because self-employed persons remain barred by Labor Department interpretation from eligibility for alien labor certification, otherwise known as the PERM program. This is a step forward out of the morass, but this USCIS liberalization only impacts a small number of the most exceptional with a long-established track record attracting VC or creating successful start-ups. Younger applicants and those who have not yet risen to a position of prominence will find it difficult to qualify for a NIW. Eligibility for the upper employment-based preference categories, EB-1 and EB-2, are interpreted very strictly, so strictly in fact that the 9th Circuit Court of Appeals found in the Kazarian decision2 that USCIS adjudicators were adding substantive requirements to

1 USCIS, Employment-Based Second Preference Immigrant Visa Category, Frequently Asked Questions Regarding Entrepreneurs and the Employment-Based Second Preference Immigrant Visa Category. http://www.uscis.gov/portal/site/uscis/menuitem.5af9bb95919f35e66f614176543f6d1a/?vgnextoid=93da6b814ba81310VgnVCM100000082ca60aRCRD&vgnextchannel=6abe6d26d17df110VgnVCM1000004718190aRCRD.

2*Kazarian v USCIS*, 596 F3d 1115 (9th Cir., March 4, 2010), http://www.ca9.uscourts.gov/datastore/opinions/2010/03/04/07-56774.pdf

EB-1 above and beyond those found in the regulations to make eligibility for Outstanding Ability Researchers even more restrictive.

Any applicant with an advanced degree who is published extensively, has held a university teaching position or holds patents on scientific or technological discoveries should be eligible.

- The requirement that the applicant shows superiority to Americans in the same field must be eliminated.

The EB-1 extraordinary category is available to persons have risen to the highest echelons of their respective fields of expertise applicants who have been the recipient of prizes and awards for outstanding achievement in those fields. Meanwhile EB-2 National Interest Waiver requirements remain so elevated that only a small percentage of entrepreneurs and applicants in other fields may qualify. The extremely restrictive criteria imposed by administrative edict must be recalibrated in favor of more extensive outreach to highly qualified applicants of all kinds.

6. DHS

The Department of Homeland Security, which has already become a well-entrenched, massive bureaucracy rivaling the Pentagon, needs a massive overhaul. At the crux of the legal immigration mess are problems with adjudicators in the Exams Sections of USCIS Service Centers who are permitted to apply standards that exceed those contained in the lawful regulations. Some of that problem is institutional entrenchment, while another is the adjudicators themselves and the quality of their decisions. Currently, adjudicators are hired based on less-than-stringent standards. New hires should include candidates with Masters Degrees or higher, candidates well-educated and trained in the specifics of immigration policies and practices.

The current culture of "No" and "Not on my watch" must evolve into a methodology that asks, "What can we do to approve this application?" Today, it is much easier (and to the bureaucrat mired in bureaucracy, much safer) to simply deny applications despite the exceptional promise of the individual beneficiary contained within them.

Until we alter the quality of perceptions of those people responsible for immigration decisions, we will not be able to solve our immigration mess. No matter what law Congress passes, each agency must possess the mission of implementing the intent of Congress, rather than thwarting it. Our administrators must embrace the culture of potential rather than hide in the comfort of inertia.

7. Visa Eligibility

The current system permits just over one million visas per year, 80% of which are in the amorphous category of "family visas," visas based on qualifying eligibility gained from a spouse, parent or sibling who resides in the U.S. If a choice must be made, and Congress will not increase numbers, this category should be *reduced*, thereby releasing more visas for exceptional, extraordinary, entrepreneurial and investor visas.

The over-emphasis on family reunification seems a noble goal but, frankly, does not significantly benefit the United States as dramatically as other visas. Family visas require no special qualifications or skills other than being related by marriage to someone residing in the U.S. While bringing families together is an important goal, we must also take a long hard look at the ways we can best benefit families already in the U.S. The family-based immigration preference system was designed in a time when quantity of labor, the number of hands who could operate an immigrant family-run laundry or dry cleaning store, counted for more than the quality of education and technical expertise each brought into creating and building a competitive business.

8. Create a Basic Worker Category

While it's vital to establish more and better visa categories for exceptional and entrepreneurial people, it is equally important to provide opportunities for the people who will cut our grass, pick our crops, care for our children and elderly, and any number of other jobs that require minimal education. Under current law, it is virtually impossible to qualify these workers for green cards.

While not considered high-skill, people willing to fill these occupations will continue to be an essential part of our society.

On A Personal Note:

As an Immigration specialist, I can't tell you how many thousands of calls my practice received requesting help finding service workers — a nanny, a chef, gardeners and cleaners — from professional couples, each of whom worked 6 days a week and had no one they could count on to arrive on time, reliably tend to tasks, and safely look after their kids. Given the overwhelming, ongoing demand for labor in these areas, it is absurd that the U.S. doesn't allocate but a handful of visas for such workers, and then after a decade or more wait. It is equally bizarre that we intentionally make our own lives, lives of hard-working U.S. citizens, that much harder when there is no justifiable reason for doing so.

Conclusion

Our immigration policies are seriously flawed and these problems make our society less healthy than it could be. Americans need to adopt these simple steps to grow our economy and kick start our standard of living to new heights by again embracing our heritage as a nation of Immigrants.

INDEX

Made in the USA
Middletown, DE
07 December 2020